MOUNTAINS
OF
THE WORLD

▲ A Handbook for Climbers & Hikers ▲

by WILLIAM M. BUELER

THE MOUNTAINEERS
Seattle, Washington

THE MOUNTAINEERS . . . Organized 1906

*" . . . to explore, study, preserve and enjoy
the natural beauty of Northwest America . . . "*

TABLE OF CONTENTS

LIST OF MAPS

A note from the publisher:

When this book was first published, by the Charles E. Tuttle Co., Inc. of Tokyo in 1970, most hikers and climbers had been confining their activities to their own countries. Within the last several years, however, there has been a seeming explosion of interest in exploring peaks in the less well known areas of the world. As a service, then, to these far-ranging mountain travelers, The Mountaineers have republished William Bueler's unique and comprehensive book on what are truly the "high points" of the world.

In his original preface, Mr. Bueler introduces some cautions and considerations in the use of this book. To these must be added another: political events in the intervening years in some countries have made some of the information no longer completely accurate (even some of the country names may have changed), and individuals and local organizations named in the text may have been superseded.

Readers who are aware of updated information and/or who have material on other interesting mountains not described here are encouraged to forward this information to the author, in care of the publisher.

THE MOUNTAINEERS

PREFACE

This handbook has several features. First, it is world-wide in scope; it includes out-of-the-way peaks and ranges for which information is difficult to obtain, in addition to such familiar areas as the Alps, Rockies, and Andes. Second, the book concentrates largely on the highest summits in each region, although some information on other interesting peaks and rock-climbing areas is also included. I have emphasized the highest summits because I feel they are of the greatest general interest (although not necessarily, of course, of the greatest intrinsic interest to mountaineers); also, since it is impossible to give thorough and detailed coverage to every mountain area in the world in a book like this, there is no choice but to limit the coverage to the "high spots"—whether literally or figuratively. In many cases I have indicated where additional, more detailed information can be obtained. Third, the book describes the mountains primarily from the point of view of the hiker or casual, nonexpert mountaineer; the route descriptions in almost all cases are for the "normal route"—i.e., the easiest route.

Because of the focus on the normal routes, I have not found it practical to use numerical difficulty ratings; instead, verbal descriptions are used. For instance, "moderate" rock climbing, as on the easiest routes up the Grand Teton and the Matterhorn, could be done by a strong hiker with a professional guide or other fully qualified leader; but "difficult" rock climbing, as on Mt. Kenya, or "difficult" snow and ice climbing, as on Mt. Cook, would demand that all members of a party be experienced in roped climbing. Climbing on glaciers is frequently quite easy, as on the normal routes up some of the volcanoes of Washington State or Ecuador, but any glacier travel has dangers which make it imperative that novices not attempt it without a fully qualified leader or guide. To the experienced alpinist, the large number of climbs that are described as "rock scrambles" will just be carefree romps, but the lowlander new to the mountains who encounters a steep grade and a little exposure may feel as though he is scaling the Eigerwand. Therefore, hikers or beginning climbers should have a modicum of mountain experience before tackling on their own any of the peaks which involve "rock scrambling."

Anyone interested in the mountains of the world must also be interested in the geography of the world, and he will certainly own a reasonably good atlas. Therefore, general maps are not included in the handbook. For the route descriptions I have tried in almost all cases to relate the starting point to some place identifiable in the *National Geographic Atlas of the World*.

WILLIAM M. BUELER

ACKNOWLEDGMENTS

This handbook could not have been written without the help of dozens of people. Some of them are well-known mountaineers, but some are just hikers who happen to be familiar with an out-of-the-way mountain. Nevertheless, the responsibility for any errors lies wholly with the author. I would like to express my appreciation to the following people, who either responded to requests for information or read one or more chapters in draft: Ichiro Yashizawa, Wen-an Lin, Y. Yamazaki, Tae-Hung Ha, Eti Rice, Richard A. von Glatz, Nicholas B. Clinch, A. H. McCormack, Gregorio Araneta II, Brian McArdle, W. H. Biscoe, Taian Kato, Lt. Col. James Roberts, Leon M. S. Slawecki, Gen. Molavi, Manfred W. Wenner, Aryeh Louv, E. W. Hahn, Moira Bird, John H. Crook, C. W. Nicol, J. P. Hull, George Schaller, Hamish M. Brown, Mario Fantin, Nassos A. Tzartzanos, Michel Fabrikant, Michele Pandolfo, Fernando Henrique de Brito Rocha, Jose Gonzalez Folliot, Einar P. Guojohnsen, Arthur K. Willey, Jr., G. M. D. Guillaume, Cesar Morales Arnao,

Alfredo H. Brignone, Jack Bermeo, J. R. Hechtel, Evelio Echevarria, Danilo Lopez Arankowsky, Gerardo Urioste, Andres Manuel Batista Barcacel, Jose Luis Beteta, Kenneth C. Scholz, M. J. Hassell, John Hart, Dick A. Cox, Francis H. Elmore, Neal G. Guse, Dick Vandenburg, A. R. McConkie, Orrin H. Bonney, Ronald J. McCormick, Wayne P. Merry, John R. Glenn, Ray Phillips, William L. Evants, John E. Whitson, Robert F. Gerath, H. D. Greenwood, Santiago Cerredoira Casares, Bernard L. Elias, Dahl L. Zohner, E. C. Rockwell, Nicholas A. Dodge, Seiso Kamimura, Theodore L. Picco, Theodore R. Jaeckel, Neal M. Jacques, Kazem Guilanpour, R. M. Chakravarty, W. C. Ledingham, Col. M. Koekoeh, Harvey H. Manning, J. Vin Hoeman, Dr. Neal M. Carter. Special thanks are due to my wife Lois, who more than once reviewed the entire manuscript.

MOUNTAINS
OF
THE WORLD

MAP SYMBOLS

Glacier		Cable Car	
Lake		Train (Railway)	
Stream		Peak	△
Ridge or Crest		Contour Line	
Road		Pass or Col	
Route		City, Town or Village	
Trail		Hut, Small Settlement, Shelter or Building(s)	□
Track		Campground or Base Camp	⊕

16

▲ EASTERN UNITED STATES ▲

All the major mountains of the eastern United States except the Adirondacks are part of the Appalachian chain, which extends for 1200 miles from Georgia to Maine. For the most part the mountains are wooded all the way to their tops, but in New England the highest summits rise well above timberline.

The highest peak in the eastern United States is Mt. Mitchell (6684 feet) in the Blue Ridge Mountains of North Carolina. A road leads to within a few minutes' walk of its top, on which there is an observation tower. For hikers, there is a five-and-a-half mile trail to the summit from the Black Mountain Campground, which is reached by a four-mile turnoff from the Blue Ridge Parkway.

Slightly lower than Mt. Mitchell is Clingmans Dome (6642 feet), the highest peak in Tennessee, and the highest in Great Smoky Mountains National Park. The observation tower on its summit can be reached in a short walk from the Forney Ridge Parking Area.

The Adirondack Mountains of New York are crowned by the rocky summit of Mt. Marcy (5347 feet). There are five trails up Mt. Marcy, the shortest of which—seven miles one-way—begins north of the mountain at Adirondack Lodge. There are a total of 46 peaks over 4000 feet in the Adirondacks.

The most impressive mountains in the eastern U. S. are those of New England, where the highest peak is 6288-foot Mt. Washington in the White Mountains of New Hampshire. Mt. Washington's summit is reached by an automobile road, a cog railway, and several trails, of which the Tuckerman Ravine Trail from Pinkham Notch (2030 feet) is one of the most scenic and most popular. Despite its low elevation compared with our western mountains, Mt. Washington rises about 1000 feet above timberline and is a big mountain with all the dangers inherent in big mountains. Among its distinctions it claims (1) the world's highest recorded wind velocity—231 miles per hour, and (2) perhaps the greatest death toll of any mountain in the United States—over 50 people, many of whom were inexperienced hikers unprepared for the violent changes in the weather.

The highest summit in Maine, 5268-foot Mt. Katahdin, can be climbed by a 2050-mile-long trail (walking time about one summer), which begins in Georgia. Or, if you don't have time to walk the full length of the Appalachian Trail, you can cut off the first 2044.8 miles, and join the trail at Katahdin Stream Campground on the west side of the mountain. Mt. Katahdin rises well above timberline and its cirques and narrow ridges offer the most alpine scenery and climbing in the eastern U. S. Including Katahdin, Maine claims 12 summits over 4000 feet; added to the 46 of New Hampshire and the five of Vermont, this makes a total of 63 for New England.

New England has numerous rock-climbing areas. The greatest rock wall in the East is the east face of New Hampshire's Cannon Mountain; this face is almost 1000 feet high and the climbing has been likened to that of a small-scale Yosemite wall. Other popular eastern rock-climbing centers include the Shawangunk Mountains, about 50 miles northwest of New York City, and Seneca Rock, about 15 miles northwest of Petersburg, West Virginia. In fact, rock enthusiasts can find cliffs or rock domes scattered up and down the entire length of the Appalachians, beginning with Stone Mountain on the outskirts of Atlanta. Of the states in the southern portion of the range, North Carolina is particularly well endowed in this regard.

▲ TEXAS ▲

The existence of two national parks set aside to preserve the mountain scenery of Texas is convincing proof that the state has something other than flatland and sagebrush. The highest mountain in the state is 8751-foot Guadalupe Peak, which is the dominant feature of Guadalupe Mountains National Park, just south of the New Mexico border. On the south side of the peak is the vertical-walled buttress called "El Capitan," one of the most spectacular natural features in the state. The starting point for the climb up Guadalupe Peak is just west of Guadalupe Pass on U. S. Highway 62-180. From this spot, which is south of the peak at 5200 feet, there is a poorly defined trail about three-and-a-half miles long to the summit.

Big Bend National Park is known primarily for the gorge at the big bend of the Rio Grande, but it also contains the Chisos Mountains, which are an interesting desert range with steep cliffs, spectacular rock formations, and—like the Guadalupes—refreshing stands of conifer forest. The highest peak is 7835-foot Emory Peak.

Halfway between the Guadalupe Mountains and the Chisos Mountains are the Davis Mountains, topped by 8382-foot Mt. Livermore.

▲ NEW MEXICO ▲

The mountains of New Mexico are not as alpine as those of the northern Rocky Mountain states, of course, but there is more mountain scenery in the state than is usually recognized. The highest peaks are in the Sangre de Cristo Range of north-central New Mexico, where Wheeler Peak (13,160 feet) tops a number of other summits only slightly lower. Wheeler Peak is 13 miles northeast of Taos. The usual route up Wheeler begins at Twining (9300 feet), a ski area where there are several

MAP 1. WHEELER PEAK, New Mexico

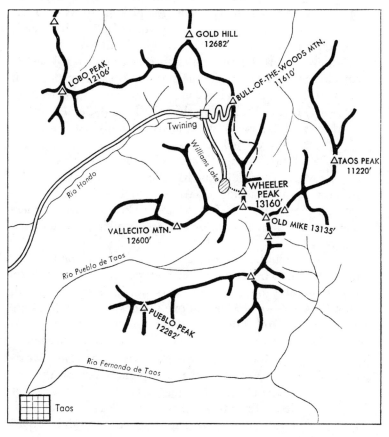

△ GOLD HILL
12682′

LOBO PEAK
12106′

BULL-OF-THE-WOODS MTN.
11610′

Twining

Williams Lake

Rio Hondo

△ TAOS PEAK
11220′

WHEELER
PEAK
13160′

△ OLD MIKE 13135′

VALLECITO MTN.
12600′

Rio Pueblo de Taos

△ PUEBLO PEAK
12282′

Rio Fernando de Taos

Taos

Scale 0   1   2   3   4   5 mi.

lodges and a campground. The most popular route is by way of an old mining road (passable for pickup trucks or other vehicles with good clearance) to the top of Bull-of-the-Woods Mountain; here one joins Forest Service Trail No. 290, which is followed south for five miles to the summit of Wheeler. An alternative route is up the steep west slope of the peak from Williams Lake (11,000 feet). Also over 13,000 feet are the four Truchas Peaks—South, Middle, West, and North— of which 13,102-foot South Truchas is the highest. The steep rock faces of West Truchas offer some of the most challenging technical climbs among the state's higher mountains.

New Mexico's most frequently climbed range is the Sandia Mountains just outside of Albuquerque. Though a road reaches the top of 10,678-foot Sandia Crest, the range offers many opportunities both for wilderness hiking and for rock climbing.

For rock climbers, however, New Mexico's main attractions are not to be found on the high peaks, but in the desert —most notably on 7178-foot Shiprock. This great volcanic plug rises a sheer 1700 feet above the desert of northwestern New Mexico, and is in fact one of the most impressive peaks in the U.S. The Indians have closed Shiprock to climbing.

The Organ Mountains, just east of Las Cruces, New Mexico, and north of El Paso, Texas, are perhaps America's most impressive desert range. Their jagged crestline rises 5000 feet above the desert floor to an elevation of 9012 feet in Organ Needle. Several peaks in the range require rope, while Organ Needle itself is a very steep scramble.

Climbers in New Mexico will find Herbert E. Ungnade's *Guide to the New Mexico Mountains* very useful.

▲ ARIZONA ▲

Although Arizona is noted less for its mountains than for its canyons, the state's climbers do not have any trouble finding things to do. Arizona's loftiest summit is Humphreys Peak (12,633 feet), which is the highest point on the rim of a huge, long-dead volcano. The volcano itself is a great hulk known as San Francisco Mountain—or the San Francisco Peaks, since there are three main summits. Based on the size of what remains of the volcano's lower slopes, geologists have estimated that San Francisco Mountain at one time may have reached 15,000 feet, which is higher than any present-day peak in the U. S. outside of Alaska. Humphreys Peak is only 10 miles north of Flagstaff and is an easy one-day hike from the Arizona Snow Bowl Lodge on the west side of the mountain at 9500 feet. One hikes to the upper terminal of the chair lift at 11,600 feet, from where the route follows a high saddle to the north for about a mile to the highest summit. The mountain rises over 1000 feet above timberline and patches of snow last well into the summer.

After the San Francisco Peaks the highest mountain in Arizona is Baldy Peak (11,590 feet), 20 miles southeast of Mc-Nary. It is an easy climb, as are a number of other peaks over 9000 feet which dot the eastern half of Arizona. For technical climbers the high peaks of Arizona do not offer a great deal,

MAP 2. HUMPHREYS PEAK, ARIZONA

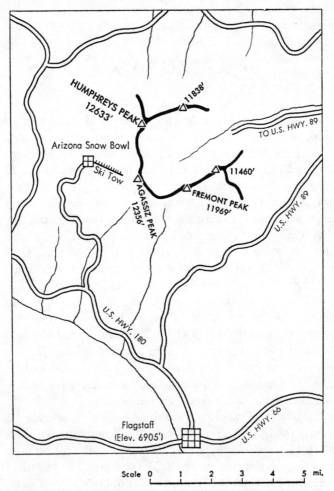

HUMPHREYS PEAK
12633'

11838'

TO U.S. HWY. 89

Arizona Snow Bowl

Ski Tow

11460'

AGASSIZ PEAK
12356'

FREMONT PEAK
11969'

U.S. HWY. 89

U.S. HWY. 180

Flagstaff
(Elev. 6905')

U.S. HWY. 66

Scale 0   1   2   3   4   5 mi.

but the airy monoliths of the state's deserts and canyons are a different matter. Within the Grand Canyon itself are formations—such as Vishnu Temple, Shiva Temple, and Wotan's Throne—which fully deserve to be considered mountains, and which present considerably greater climbing problems than most of the West's high peaks. Yet one looks down on their summits from the rim of the Canyon.

From the rock climber's standpoint one of the most interesting mountains in Arizona is Agathla Peak (7100 feet), a needlelike volcanic plug at the southern end of Monument Valley. It rises 1200 feet above its base, and is as steep, though not quite as high, as New Mexico's Shiprock. The vertical-walled buttes and monoliths of Monument Valley itself have also become goals for desert rock climbers in recent years. Climbers must take care to respect Indian regulations regarding climbing in this area.

▲ COLORADO ▲

Colorado is truly "High Country, U.S.A." Of the approximately 68 peaks in the U. S. excluding Alaska that exceed 14,000 feet, 53 are in Colorado. Furthermore, three-fourths of the total area over 10,000 feet elevation in the contiguous United States is in this state, which has an average elevation of 6800 feet.

Colorado's highest peak, and the highest in the entire

Rocky Mountains, is 14,433-foot Mt. Elbert, southwest of Leadville. For the most common route up Elbert one begins at a point half a mile west of the Halfmoon Campground (10,000 feet) on Highway 300, and follows the Main Range Trail southward for two miles to where it crosses the northeast ridge of the peak. From here, it is an easy climb of three miles up the ridge to the summit. The top of Mt. Elbert was used as a triangulation point by the Hayden Survey in the 1870's, but the mountain had probably been climbed by Indians or trappers several decades earlier. Well over half of Colorado's 14,000-foot peaks can, like Elbert, be climbed by walking routes. These include Mt. Massive (14,421 feet), Mt. Harvard (14,420 feet), La Plata Peak (14,336 feet), Blanca Peak (14,317 feet), and Uncompahgre Peak (14,309 feet)—the 2nd, 3rd, 4th, 5th and 6th highest peaks in the state.

Colorado's—and America's—most famous mountain is 14,110-foot Pikes Peak, the 32nd highest in the state. The peak has both an auto road and a cog railway to its summit, and for hikers there is also a good trail. The 24-mile round-trip hike begins at the edge of Manitou Springs at 6500 feet and is often made in one day, but it is a long one. By taking the incline railway up Mt. Manitou the altitude gain can be reduced by some 2000 feet. Pikes Peak was first climbed by Edwin James and two other members of Major Long's expedition, in 1820.

After Pike's Peak, Colorado's next best-known mountain is Longs Peak (14,256 feet), the king of Rocky Mountain National Park. The regular route of ascent begins at the Longs Peak Campground (9400 feet), from where a trail leads six miles to Boulder Field (12,600 feet). Continue to the Key-

MAP 3. MT. ELBERT and MT. MASSIVE, COLORADO

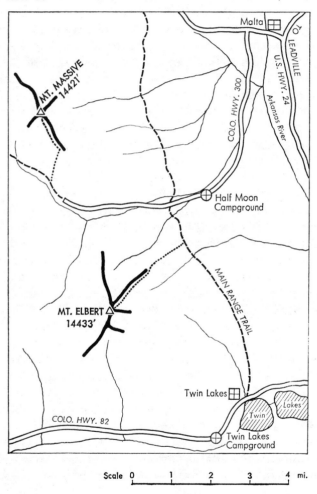

hole Ridge. The route is then well marked with yellow and red bull's eyes. The east face of Longs Peak is a vertical, 1700-foot-high wall that has been the scene of much spectacular rock climbing. The first recorded ascent of Longs Peak was made in 1868 by the party of Major Powell (who later won fame as the first man to go through the Grand Canyon on a boat down the Colorado River); however there is evidence of earlier ascents by Indians, probably for the purpose of making signal fires or trapping eagles

Although all the above mentioned peaks as well as many others of Colorado's "14's" can be climbed without technical difficulty, the state also has several areas with more challenging peaks, particularly the Elk Range near Aspen, the Sangre de Cristo Range in the south-central part of Colorado, and the San Juan Mountains in the southwestern corner of the state. Rope should be carried on the major peaks in all three of these ranges. In the Elks, Capitol Peak (14,130 feet) is a granite mountain whose steep walls and knife-edge ridges offer no easy way up, making it perhaps the most difficult of Colorado's 14,000-foot peaks. Pyramid Peak (14,018 feet), Maroon Peak (14,156 feet), and North Maroon Peak (14,014 feet) are all rather demanding scrambles on fractured sandstone. In the Sangre de Cristos, Kit Carson Peak (14,165 feet), Crestone Peak (14,294 feet), and Crestone Needle (14,191 feet) are spectacular rock peaks requiring rugged scrambling on firm conglomerate. In the San Juans there are a number of interesting scrambles on mountains just over 14,000 feet, while several slightly lower peaks are among the state's most challenging climbs; Arrow Peak (13,803 feet) and Vestal Peak (13,846 feet) in the Grenadier Range of the

MAP 4. PIKES PEAK, COLORADO

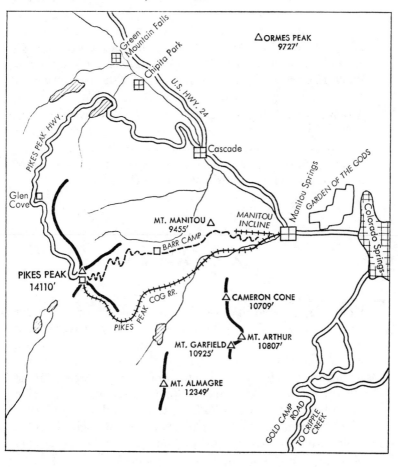

△ ORMES PEAK
9727'

Green Mountain Falls

Chipita Park

U.S. HWY. 24

PIKES PEAK HWY.

Cascade

Manitou Springs

GARDEN OF THE GODS

Glen Cove

Colorado Springs

MT. MANITOU △
9455'

MANITOU
INCLINE

BARR CAMP

PIKES PEAK
14110'

PIKES PEAK COG RR.

PIKES

△ CAMERON CONE
10709'

MT. GARFIELD △
10925'

△ MT. ARTHUR
10807'

△ MT. ALMAGRE
12349'

GOLD CAMP ROAD

TO CRIPPLE CREEK

Scale 0   1   2   3   4 mi.

San Juans are perhaps the most difficult major mountains in the state to climb.

Although hikers and rock climbers can each find a lifetime of enjoyment in the Colorado mountains, snow and ice climbers will have to head farther north. There are only a few small glaciers, and these are primarily in the northern part of the state, in or near Rocky Mountain National Park. Timberline in Colorado averages about 11,500 feet.

A good guidebook, Robert Ormes' *Guide to the Colorado Mountains,* gives route descriptions to all the state's highest summits. Another is *The Colorado Fourteens — A Condensed Guide,* published by The Colorado Mountain Club.

▲ UTAH ▲

Utah, like Arizona, is better known for its canyons than for its mountains, and between them the two states have without doubt the most spectacular and colorful canyon country on earth. But Utah also has its full share of mountains, the highest of which are the Uinta Mountains in the northeast part of the state. The Uintas claim the distinction of being the only major range in the U. S. that extends east and west. The range has a characteristic glaciated topography with steep cirques, U-shaped valleys, and a tremendous number of small lakes. Utah's highest mountain, Kings Peak (13,528 feet), is situated near the center of the range in the midst

MAP 5. KINGS PEAK, Utah

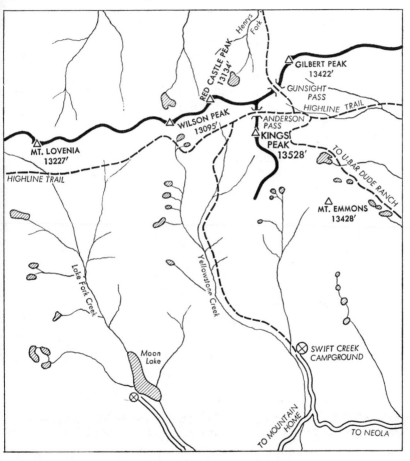

Scale 0 1 2 3 4 5 6 mi.

of a vast area of wilderness. From a technical standpoint it is an easy mountain, but its isolated location makes it a very long climb in terms of mileage. A 20-mile trail to its summit begins at Swift Creek Campground, south of the peak at about 8400 feet. The trail follows Yellowstone Creek, a tributary of the Green River, most of the way to Anderson Pass, which is about a mile north of the summit; from the campground to the pass is 19 miles. From Anderson Pass, a rocky slope leads to the highest point. Other trails approach Kings Peak from Henrys Fork on the north and Uinta Canyon on the east. In addition to Kings Peak, five other Uinta summits exceed 13,000 feet; all of them are long hikes though technically easy.

Outside of the Uintas, the highest peak in Utah is 12,721-foot Mt. Peale in the La Sal Mountains southeast of Moab. Mt. Peale is an easy hike of about three miles from La Sal Pass, which is southwest of the peak at approximately 10,000 feet; the pass is reached by a dirt road which turns off State Highway 46 some five miles northeast of the town of La Sal. The La Sal Mountains are an imposing background for some of the most amazing rock formations on earth—those of Arches National Monument and Canyonlands National Park. At the northern foot of the La Sals are the slender Fisher Towers, which are among the tallest rock needles to be found anywhere; one of them rises 900 feet above its base.

The La Sals are just one of several isolated laccolithic domes that lift their forested slopes above the red-rock desert and canyon country of southeastern Utah. Others are the Henry Mountains, which reach 11,615 feet in Mt. Ellen; the Abajo Mountains, with 11,345-foot Abajo Peak; and Navajo

Mountain (10,416 feet), at the foot of which is the world's largest natural arch, Rainbow Bridge.

The ranges and plateaus that run north to south down the middle of Utah reach 12,173 feet in Delano Peak in the Tushar Mountains. Better known is Mt. Timpanogos (11,750 feet) in the Wasatch Range; its prominent position southeast of Salt Lake City makes it the most popular mountain in the state. Timpanogos is a broad, steep-sided mountain which rises 7000 feet directly above the flat floor of the Jordan River Valley. The most common route to the summit is the five-mile trail from Aspen Grove, at about 7000 feet on the east side of the mountain. Hikers whose mountain fun lies in the enjoyment of sociability rather than wilderness can join several thousand others for the annual "Timp Hike" each July. Mt. Timpanogos rises well above timberline and on its north side there is a permanent snowfield called "Timpanogos Glacier."

▲ SOUTH DAKOTA ▲

The Black Hills are the highest mountains east of the Rockies, but that is not the only claim they have to our attention. They are beautiful mountains with much to offer both hikers and rock climbers, as well as the nearly two million tourists who come each year to see such attractions as Mt. Rushmore, which contains the colossal carved heads of Washington, Jefferson, Lincoln, and Theodore Roosevelt. The highest summit, 7242-foot Harney Peak, is reached by four trails, each starting from a different location; information about these and other trails can be obtained from one of the ranger stations of Black Hills National Forest. From the summit of Harney Peak one looks out over the nearby Needles, spectacular granite spires which offer good rock climbing.

▲ WYOMING ▲

Teton Range

Wyoming probably has more to offer the mountaineer than any other American state except Alaska. In fact, many climbers would claim that the two best climbing areas in the American West are the Teton Range and the Wind River Range, both of which are in Wyoming. The Tetons are by far the better known and more accessible of the two, and they have been admired by millions of tourists who have never even heard of the Wind Rivers. Anyone approaching Yellowstone National Park from the south passes through the broad valley called Jackson's Hole, above which the Tetons burst skyward in one majestic sweep. Few mountain scenes are more magnificent than that of the Grand Teton

MAP 6. GRAND TETON, WYOMING

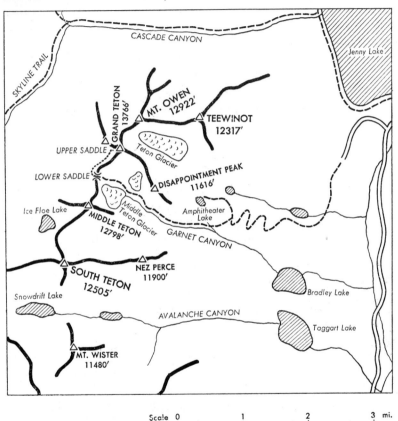

CASCADE CANYON

SKYLINE TRAIL

Jenny Lake

GRAND TETON 13766'

MT. OWEN 12922'

TEEWINOT 12317'

UPPER SADDLE

Teton Glacier

LOWER SADDLE

DISAPPOINTMENT PEAK 11616'

Ice Floe Lake

Middle Teton Glacier

MIDDLE TETON 12798'

Amphitheater Lake

GARNET CANYON

NEZ PERCE 11900'

SOUTH TETON 12505'

Snowdrift Lake

AVALANCHE CANYON

Bradley Lake

Taggart Lake

MT. WISTER 11480'

Scale 0   1   2   3 mi.

soaring fully 7000 feet above the flat floor of Jackson's Hole.

The Grand Teton is sharp peak with high walls on all sides. Even on the south, which is the approach most often used, there are nearly 2000 feet of steep rock between the Lower Saddle and the summit (the "Lower Saddle" is the low point between the Middle Teton and Grand Teton). The north face of the Grand Teton is a nearly vertical wall well over 2000 feet high, which has been the scene of some of the most impressive climbs in the range. There is no easy route up the Grand Teton, and even the least difficult, the Owen-Spalding route, requires an experienced leader and the use of a rope. However, there is a mountaineering school at Jenny Lake in Grand Teton National Park which will assist strong hikers without previous technical experienced to make the climb. First the novice climber completes a one-day course in mountaineering techniques, after which he can make the two-day summit climb with a guide from the school; equipment can also be rented from the school. In climbing the Grand Teton, parties usually hike up Garnet Canyon to the Lower Saddle (11,644 feet) on the first day, and climb to the summit and return to Jackson's Hole on the second.

The first ascent of the Grand Teton was probably that of two members of the Hayden Survey, N. P. Langford and James Stevenson, in 1872. Interestingly enough, prior to that date the Indians had already reached the peak's western spur, a few hundred feet below the summit, where they had constructed a shelter. Langford was told by a local Indian woman that the Indians had tried many times to reach the highest summit, but without success. However, the Indians

MAP 7.   GANNETT PEAK, WYOMING

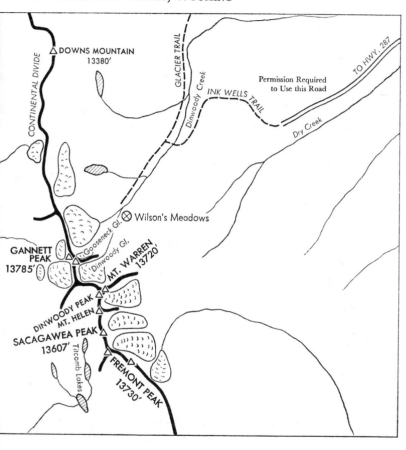

△ DOWNS MOUNTAIN
13380'

CONTINENTAL DIVIDE

GLACIER TRAIL

Dinwoody Creek

INK WELLS TRAIL

TO HWY. 287

Permission Required
to Use this Road

Dry Creek

⊗ Wilson's Meadows

Gooseneck Gl.

Dinwoody Gl.

GANNETT
PEAK
13785'

MT. WARREN
13720'

DINWOODY PEAK
MT. HELEN △

SACAGAWEA PEAK
13607'

Titcomb Lakes

FREMONT PEAK
13730'

Scale   0   1   2   3   4   5   mi.

were more successful on the range's third highest peak, 12,798-foot Middle Teton, on the summit of which they left another shelter.

Aside from the Grand and Middle Tetons the peaks over 12,000 feet are Mt. Owen (12,922 feet), Mt. Moran (12,594 feet), South Teton (12,505 feet), Teewinot (12,317 feet), and Thor Peak (12,018 feet). Of these South Teton offers perhaps the least difficult route, but still requires an experienced leader and a rope. Mt. Owen is considered the most difficult major peak in the range. The highest walk-up in the range is probably Mt. Woodring (11,585 feet), while Buck Mountain (11,923 feet) is often considered a good climb for beginning mountaineers.

The climbing season in the Tetons is usually mid-June to mid-September, with August offering the best climbing conditions. There are a number of small glaciers in the Tetons, but they are smaller than those of the Wind Rivers, although the Tetons are farther north. Timberline in the Tetons is approximately 10,000 feet. Two guidebooks cover the Tetons in detail: *A Climber's Guide to the Teton Range,* by Leigh Ortenburger; and *Guide to the Wyoming Mountains and Wilderness Areas,* by O. H. Bonney.

Wind River Range

Though the Tetons are the most popular climbing range in Wyoming, if not in the entire country, Wyoming's other great range, the Wind Rivers, is thought by some climbers to have even more to offer. The Wind Rivers have the most extensive glaciers in the American Rocky Mountains, and rock climbing comparable to that of the Tetons, all in one of the vastest tracts of roadless wilderness in the contiguous United States. For good measure, Gannett Peak (13,785 feet) in the Wind Rivers tops the Grand Teton by 19 feet and is the highest in Wyoming. The northern portion of the Wind Rivers contains all the large glaciers and all the range's peaks of 13,500 feet or more; these are, in addition to Gannett, Fremont Peak (13,730 feet), Mt. Warren (13,720 feet), Mt. Sacagawea (13,607 feet), Mt. Helen (13,600 feet), Doublet Peak (13,600 feet), Mt. Woodrow Wilson (13,500 feet), East Sentinel (13,500 feet), and Turret (13,500 feet).

The usual base for climbing Gannett Peak is Wilson Meadows, which is northeast of the summit at 10,000 feet. The meadows can be reached in one very long day or two short days via the Ink Wells Trail, which begins at the end of a dirt road that turns off U.S. Highway 287 two miles north of Burris; however, permission must be obtained from the local Indian tribes. Otherwise, one can take the Glacier Trail which begins at the end of a road which turns off Highway 287 four miles southeast of Dubois; the Glacier Trail approach, which goes by way of Trail Lake, is five miles longer than the Ink Wells Trail approach. From Wilson Meadows the route follows Dinwoody Creek, then crosses Dinwoody and Gooseneck glaciers, and finally skirts to the right of Gooseneck Pinnacle before reaching the peak's distinctive summit snowcap. This route is a moderate ice and rock climb, requiring rope and ice axe. The first verified ascent of Gannett was that of Arthur Tate and Floyd Stahlnaker in 1922.

Fremont Peak, the second highest in the range, can be

climbed without a rope from Island Lake to the west, but it is a rough scramble and inexperienced climbers may want the rope. Credit for the first ascent of Fremont Peak has usually been given to John C. Fremont, the famous Army explorer, for a climb in 1842; however, O. H. Bonney, in the *Guide to the Wyoming Mountains and Wilderness Areas,* argues that Fremont's description of the ascent more accurately fits Mt. Woodrow Wilson. Fremont's party included one Johnie Janisse, who was probably the first Negro to climb a major mountain in the United States. Whether or not Fremont climbed the mountain that bears his name, it was certainly climbed by the Hayden expedition of 1878.

For hikers, the highest peak with a walk-up route in the northern part of the Wind Rivers is 13,400-foot Dinwoody Peak; however, ice axe and crampons should be taken. Another interesting mountain suitable for hiking parties is Wind River Peak (13,225 feet) at the southern end of the range. This peak was the highest one visible from the Oregon Trail as travelers approached the Continental Divide in the early days of the West; thus it bears the name of the whole range. There are good rock climbs to be found throughout the Wind Rivers, most notably in the southern part of the range where the jagged granite pinnacles of the Cirque of the Towers offer some of the best rock climbing in the country. Timberline in the Wind Rivers averages about 10,600 feet.

Other Wyoming Ranges

The third major range in Wyoming is the Bighorn Mountains in the north-central part of the state. The highest mountain,

13,165-foot Cloud Peak, is a rugged rock scramble requiring two or three days round trip from the end of a poor dirt road that turns off U.S. Highway 16, some 14 miles west of Buffalo. In 1887 the first white party to reach the summit of Cloud Peak found the remains of an Indian shelter on the summit. In the Bighorns there are several peaks over 12,000 feet which have no nontechnical routes. At 13,000 feet, Mt. Woolsey, the third highest, is a fairly difficult rock climb; its slightly higher neighbor, 13,014-foot Black Tooth, is somewhat easier, though rope should be taken. Timberline in the Bighorns is about 10,000 feet. There are several small glaciers in the range.

North of the Wind Rivers and east of Yellowstone is another major range, the Absaroka Range. The highest summit, Francs Peak (13,140 feet), is an easy hike of 16 miles round trip from the old mining town of Kerwin, which is reached by a jeep road from Meeteetsee.

One of the most unusual "mountains" in the United States is Devils Tower, a vertical-walled volcanic plug which juts 900 feet above the plains of eastern Wyoming; it is a favorite goal of rock climbers.

▲ MONTANA ▲

Glacier National Park

Glacier National Park has steep, colorful rock peaks, unusually beautiful lakes, innumerable high waterfalls, extensive forests, and some 60 glaciers. With all this magnificent scenery and an extensive trail system, plus the fact that most of the area is roadless wilderness, the Park is certainly one of the most ideal areas in the U. S. for hiking and backpacking.

Most of the peaks in the Park can be ascended by climbers with only a moderate level of experience, but few are easy enough to be called "walk-ups." Even on the easiest climbs the rotten and crumbly nature of the sedimentary rock calls for constant caution, while the brokenness and complexity of the ridges and faces make it very easy to stray off even the simplest routes. Because of the rotten rock, technical climbers are not particularly attracted to Glacier.

The 10,448-foot elevation of Glacier's highest peak, Mt. Cleveland, sounds unimpressive compared to elevations in the southern Rockies, but the peak rises well over 3000 feet above timberline and its nearly 4000-foot-high north face is one of the greatest cliffs in the country. The easiest route up Mt. Cleveland begins at the southern end of Waterton Lake, at 4200 feet elevation. This starting point can be reached by

MAP 8. GRANITE PEAK, MONTANA

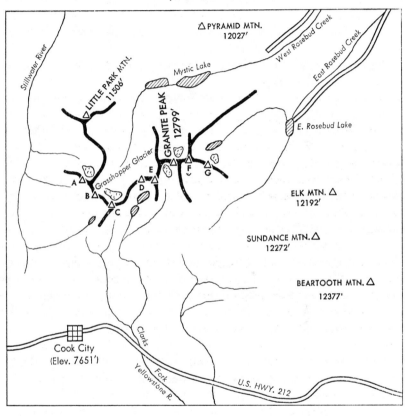

Peaks not Named on Map

A   Wolf Mtn.

B   Sawtooth Mtn. 11489′

C   Ice Berg Peak

D   Glacier Peak 12351′

E   Mt. Villiard 12337′

F   Tempest Mtn. 12478′

G   Mt. Peal 12415′

Scale 0 1 2 3 4 5 mi.

boat from the northern, Canadian, end of the lake. From the lake, a trail heads south for two miles to Camp Creek, from where one strikes cross-country up the west slope of the mountain. The distance from the lake to the summit is approximately eight miles; the climb can be made in one long day but two are usually taken. The climb involves some rock scrambling, and a rope should be taken. Cleveland was first climbed in 1924 by a group of Sierra Club climbers.

Four other peaks in the Park exceed 10,000 feet: Mt. Stimson (10,155 feet), Kintla Peak (10,110 feet), Mt. Jackson (10,033 feet), and Mt. Siyeh (10,014 feet). Stimson is a very long climb, partly over trailless terrain, and involves moderate rock climbing; J. Gordon Edwards, in *A Climber's Guide to Glacier National Park*, describes it as "the most gruelling climb in the Park." Kintla is also long, and involves both rock and snow climbing, as well as complicated route-finding problems. Jackson is shorter (approximately 28 miles round trip) and easier, and can be climbed in two days from the parking area a little less than a mile west of Baring Creek, on the Going-to-the-Sun Road. The route-finding problems are less since the upper portion is primarily a ridge climb, but there is some rock scrambling on the ridge. Mt. Siyeh is the shortest and easiest of the 10,000-foot peaks. From the Siyeh Creek curve, three miles east of Logan Pass on the Going-to-the-Sun Road at 5900 feet, it is about six miles to the summit; it is a one-day climb which involves rock scrambling.

For less ambitious hikers, 8100-foot Mt. Oberlin is the shortest and easiest big-peak-climb in the Park. The summit can be reached in about two hours from the parking area at

Logan Pass (6664 feet). The most difficult climbs in the Park include Mt. Merritt (9954 feet), Blackfoot Mountain (9607 feet), Mt. St. Nicholas (9380 feet), Mt. Wilbur (9303 feet), and Kinnerly Peak (9810 feet), all of which require rope. Of these, the steep spirelike Mt. St. Nicholas is considered the most difficult single peak.

Seen from the east, 9066-foot Chief Mountain is one of the most extraordinary mountain sights in the U.S. Its 1500-foot-high nearly perpendicular east face rises directly from the plains, and the peak stands in complete isolation well to the east of the main range. Via the somewhat gentler west face, however, Chief Mountain is only a rock scramble. When Henry L. Stimson, who later served as Secretary of State under Hoover and Secretary of War under Franklin Roosevelt, made the "first ascent" of Chief Mountain in 1891, he was intrigued to find the skull of a bison, which had presumably been put there by some unsung Indian brave. Several other first ascents in the Park are also credited to Stimson.

Beartooths

The highest mountain in Montana is 12,799-foot Granite Peak, the steep-walled monarch of the Beartooth Mountains. Granite Peak can be climbed in two or three days from either East Rosebud Lake or the end of the road up West Rosebud Creek. The usual route is by way of the divide between East and West Rosebud creeks to the pass between Granite Peak and Mt. Tempest, then up Granite's east ridge. The ridge is a roped rock climb, and a few tricky snow pitches may also be encountered early in the season. Granite Peak was first climbed in 1923 by Elers Koch and party.

The Beartooth Mountains are a wilderness of high peaks, 25 of which are over 12,000 feet. Among the major alpine regions of the U.S. it is one of the least visited, but there are limitless opportunities for both hiking and rock climbing. For technical enthusiasts, the northeast side of 12,351-foot Glacier Peak has perhaps the greatest rock wall in the range.

▲ IDAHO ▲

America's two largest designated wilderness areas are the Idaho and the Selway-Bitterroot (which is mostly in Idaho but extends into Montana). Each area is almost twice as large as Rhode Island. In neither area are the mountains especially high—they reach just over 10,000 feet—but there are no better regions anywhere for hikers and backpackers to escape civilization for weeks on end.

The highest mountain in Idaho is 12,665-foot Borah Peak in the Lost River Range. Borah can be climbed in one day from the end of the road to Birch Spring (7300 feet), on the west side of the mountain; the road turns off U.S. Highway 93A approximately 20 miles north of the town of Mackay. The walking distance to the summit is about eight miles. The route follows the west ridge to a 12,000-foot subpeak,

MAP 9.   BORAH PEAK, IDAHO

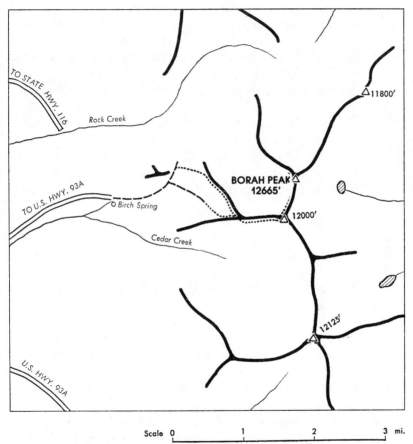

TO STATE HWY. 116

Rock Creek

△ 11800'

TO U.S. HWY. 93A

○ Birch Spring

BORAH PEAK
12665' △

△ 12000'

Cedar Creek

U.S. HWY. 93A

△ 12125'

Scale 0   1   2   3 mi.

then heads north across a saddle to the main summit. The west ridge involves some rock scrambling, and a rope (and ice axes in early summer) should be taken if inexperienced climbers are in the party. Timberline is at about 9500 feet. There has been very little rock climbing on Borah Peak because of the badly decomposed nature of the rock.

The Sawtooth Mountains, about 40 miles northwest of Sun Valley, Idaho, can claim some of the country's most spectacular alpine scenery. Though not among the highest mountains in the West—they reach only 10,776 feet in Thompson Peak—the sharp granite peaks and aiguilles of this appropriately named range make it one of America's best rock-climbing areas.

▲ NEVADA ▲

Almost all of Nevada lies within the Great Basin, which is basically a desert. But, far from flat, Nevada probably has a greater number of separate and identifiable mountain ranges than any other state in the country. The great number is accounted for by the fact that all of them are small and sufficiently isolated from each other by stretches of desert to be considered separate entities. Structurally the Great Basin ranges are fault blocks which have been squeezed upward by pressure from the east and west. A look at the map

MAP 10. WHEELER PEAK, NEVADA

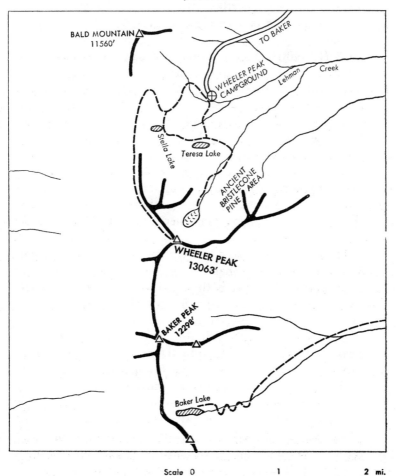

BALD MOUNTAIN 11560'

TO BAKER

WHEELER PEAK CAMPGROUND

Lehman   Creek

Stella Lake

Teresa Lake

ANCIENT BRISTLECONE PINE AREA

WHEELER PEAK 13063'

BAKER PEAK 12298'

Baker Lake

Scale   0   1   2 mi.

of Nevada reveals a neat pattern of narrow, parallel ranges all laid out along a north-south axis, and no single dominant chain breaks the pattern.

The location of the highest mountain in Nevada, Boundary Peak (13,140 feet), is sort of a fluke. By rights Boundary's summit should belong to California, since it is the northernmost peaklet of California's White Mountains. The summit is less than half a mile inside Nevada, and though the highest in that state, it is overshadowed by its 320-foot-higher neighbor, Montgomery Peak, which is just inside California. The usual starting point for climbing Boundary Peak is the end of a dirt road which turns up Trail Canyon from Nevada State Highway 3A; cars are left at about 8500 feet. The one-day summit climb is over rough trailless country (despite the name of the canyon), but there are no technical difficulties.

The second highest mountain in Nevada is 13,063-foot Wheeler Peak in the Snake Range, just a few miles from the Utah border. Wheeler is the outstanding peak in the state and ranks among the major mountains of the country. Its north face is a nearly vertical wall 1800 feet high, at the base of which is the only glacier in the Great Basin region. Wheeler Peak is not difficult to climb by the normal route, which is a five-mile trail from Wheeler Peak Campground, north of the peak at 9600 feet. The trail ascends the northwest ridge, skirting the north wall. The Snake Range is heavily forested up to a timberline of about 10,500 feet; particularly noteworthy are some of the finest extant stands of bristlecone pine. Aside from Wheeler Peak, the range has several other peaks which should be of interest to climbers, and the whole area is a wilderness that is ideal for hiking and backpacking.

Outside of the White Mountain and Snake ranges, no other Nevada mountains reach 12,000 feet, though a number of other "desert alpine islands" climb to above timberline, which ranges from 10,000 to 11,000 feet. The third highest range in the state is the Spring Mountains just 30 miles west of Las Vegas; their loftiest summit is 11,918-foot Charleston Peak.

Nevada will never be able to compete with some of the other western states as a field for serious mountaineering. But the challenges of ice and rock are not the only things mountains have to offer; another attribute of aesthetic importance is contrast, and in the interplay of desert and mountain Nevada has much that is of beauty and interest.

▲ CALIFORNIA ▲

Sierra Nevada

The Sierra Nevada is a great tilted fault block which rises precipitously on the east and slopes relatively gently toward the west. This prime characteristic of the range is well illustrated in 14,495-foot Mt. Whitney, the highest peak in the United States outside of Alaska. When seen from the east Whitney appears as a sharp pinnacle, and one would never guess that the summit is a broad expanse of boulders which slopes off gently to the west.

There is a good trail to the summit of Whitney which can be followed safely by persons with no previous experience in the mountains. Each year several thousand people climb the mountain, making it one of the most frequently ascended peaks in the country. The trail begins at Whitney Portal, a 13-mile drive from the town of Lone Pine in Owens Valley. The 21-mile round-trip hike is usually made in two days, with hikers spending the night at either Mirror Lake or Trail Camp. Mirror Lake is four miles up the trail and just a little below timberline; Trail Camp is two miles farther along the trail.

This highest summit in the "Old 48" is truly a mountain for everyone: even nonwalkers can reach the top on mule-back, while for rock climbers the precipitous east face offers very challenging routes. Mt. Whitney was first climbed in 1873 by A. H. Johnson, C. D. Begole, and John Lucas. Within six miles of Mt. Whitney are five more of California's 14 peaks over 14,000 feet: Mt. Williamson (14,384 feet), Mt. Russell (14,086 feet), Mt. Langley (14,042 feet), Mt. Tyndall (14,018 feet), and Mt. Muir (14,015 feet).

About 40 miles north of Mt. Whitney is the Palisade group, which contains five peaks over 14,000 feet and is generally considered to be the most alpine section of the entire range. North Palisade (14,242 feet), a steep rock peak with no easy way up, is the highest in the group. The least difficult route up the peak is probably by way of the southwest chute from Palisade Basin, but it requires a rope. Palisade Glacier, on the north side of North Palisade, contains about one square

MAP 11. MT. WHITNEY, CALIFORNIA

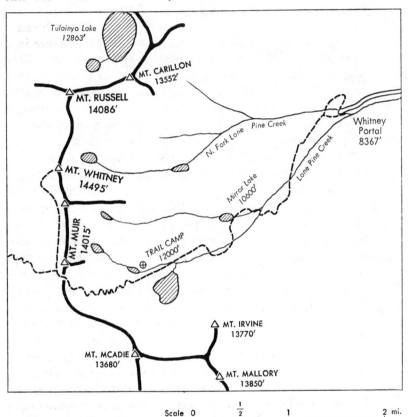

Tulainyo Lake
12863'

MT. CARILLON
13552'

MT. RUSSELL
14086'

N. Fork Lone Pine Creek

Whitney
Portal
8367'

Lone Pine Creek

MT. WHITNEY
14495'

Mirror Lake
10600'

MT. MUIR 14015'

TRAIL CAMP
12000'

MT. IRVINE
13770'

MT. MCADIE
13680'

MT. MALLORY
13850'

Scale 0   ½   1   2 mi.

mile of ice and is the largest in the Sierra Nevada. North Palisade and Thunderbolt Peak (14,000 feet), which is less than half a mile to the northwest of North Palisade, are perhaps the most difficult to climb of the 68 peaks over 14,000 feet in the U.S. outside of Alaska. The other 14,000-foot peaks in the Palisade group are Mt. Sill (14,162 feet), Middle Palisade (14,040 feet), and Polemonium Peak (14,000 feet). The only other 14,000-foot peak in the Sierra Nevada is Split Mountain (14,058 feet), which is a few miles southeast of the Palisade group.

Yosemite National Park, the best-known portion of the Sierra Nevada, has two outstanding mountain attractions—Yosemite Valley and the wilderness back country. The tremendous cliffs that enclose Yosemite Valley make it one of the world's leading rock-climbing centers, and many of today's advanced climbing techniques were originally developed to overcome such Yosemite challenges as El Capitan, a massive buttress with nearly vertical walls 3400 feet high. Few if any other cliffs on earth can match El Capitan in breadth, height, and verticality. Another equally impressive feature above the flat floor of Yosemite Valley is Half Dome (8937 feet), one of the most unusually shaped mountains on earth. As its name suggests, the mountain is in the shape of a rounded dome from which it looks as though one half has been sliced away; on the "missing" side there is a sheer wall 1700 feet high. With the help of fixed cables, the rounded side of Half Dome can be climbed by nontechnical climbers. Yosemite's second attraction, the wilderness back country, is ideal for hiking, backpacking, and climbing. Mt. Lyell (13,114 feet), the highest peak in Yosemite, involves some rock scrambling and snow climbing on its easiest route, which is up the north glacier and face to the east ridge.

The Sierra Nevada are covered very thoroughly in *A Climber's Guide to the High Sierra,* by Hervey H. Voge. A separate book, *A Climber's Guide to Yosemite Valley,* by Steve Roper, covers rock climbing in the valley.

White Mountains

Just east of Owens Valley is another range, the White Mountains, which reaches almost as high as the Sierra Nevada. There is a jeep road to the summit of White Mountain Peak (14,242 feet), the highest in the range. Ordinary cars can be driven to just under 12,000 feet on this road, which goes up the south side of the mountain. To reach the road up White Mountain Peak, one passes through the Ancient Bristlecone Pine Area, which has been set aside by the National Forest Service to preserve the oldest living trees on earth—some as much as 4600 years of age.

Mt. Shasta

The big mountain of northern California is 14,161-foot Mt. Shasta, an isolated dormant volcano which soars 10,000 feet above the surrounding countryside. Shasta is the second highest peak in the Cascade Range, after Washington's Mt. Rainier. Mt. Shasta's glaciers reach down to about 10,000 feet and are the largest in California, though they cannot compare with those in the northern Cascades. Mt. Shasta is usually climbed in two days from Sand Flat, just off the Everitt Memorial Highway at approximately 6700 feet on the south side of the mountain. Parties generally spend the night at the Sierra Club's Alpine Lodge (7950 feet), at timberline. The climb from here up the south slope is not difficult, but snow remains until late summer, and crampons and ice axe are recommended.

The southernmost major peak of the Cascade Range is Mt. Lassen (10,457 feet), which erupted sporadically between 1914 and 1921, making it the most recently active volcano in the contiguous U.S.; the climb is an easy day's hike.

▲ OREGON ▲

The highest mountain in Oregon is 11,234-foot Mt. Hood, whose familiar volcanic profile caps the eastern horizon for residents of Portland, 45 miles away. The summit climb can easily be made in one day from Timberline Lodge, at 6000 feet on the south slope. There is an even and fairly gentle slope all the way from Timberline Lodge to within a few hundred feet of the summit; in early summer there is snow all the way. Though the climb is not difficult, the final slopes are steep enough to require caution, and parties should have ice axes and crampons, and should carry a rope. Mt. Hood has several steep glaciers, particularly on the north side, which offer challenging ice climbs. The mountain was

MAP 12. MT. HOOD, OREGON

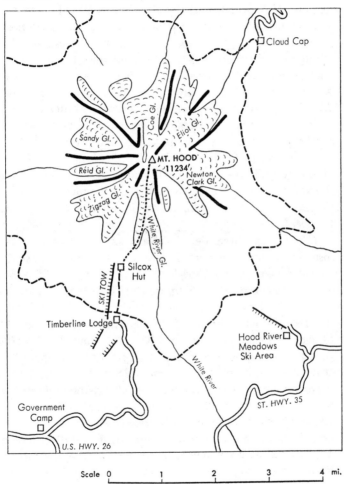

Cloud Cap

Coe Gl.

Eliot Gl.

Sandy Gl.

△MT. HOOD
11234'

Réid Gl.

Newton
Clark Gl.

Zigzag Gl.

White River Gl.

SKI TOW

Silcox
Hut

Timberline Lodge

Hood River
Meadows
Ski Area

White River

ST. HWY. 35

Government
Camp

U.S. HWY. 26

Scale 0   1   2   3   4 mi.

probably first climbed in 1857 by H. L. Pittock, L. Chittenden, W. Cornell, and the Rev. T. A. Wood.

Oregon's second highest peak is 10,495-foot Mt. Jefferson, 50 miles south of Mt. Hood. The ascent involves both glacier climbing and roped rock climbing on the summit rock pinnacle. The usual approach starts from the end of the road which turns up Whitewater Creek from State Highway 22. The climb is usually done in two days, with climbers camping overnight at Jefferson Park, a lovely valley on the north side of Mt. Jefferson. The most popular route from here goes up the Whitewater Glacier, and ends up on the northwest side of the summit pinnacle. Technically, Jefferson is probably the most difficult to climb of the great volcanoes that dot the Cascade crest from northern California to the Canadian border.

The state's three next highest summits are the Three Sisters, a compact group of extinct volcanoes to the south of Mt. Jefferson. The 10,354-foot South Sister and 10,053-foot Middle Sister have walk-up routes, but 10,058-foot North Sister has a rocky summit pinnacle similar to Mt. Jefferson's, and requires rope. For rock climbers the favorite peak in the Oregon Cascades is 7794-foot Mt. Washington, located between Mt. Jefferson and the Three Sisters; the peak is the eroded core of a pre-Pleistocene volcano.

Not so long ago, geologically speaking, the highest mountain in Oregon was Mt. Mazama, a volcano something over 12,000 feet in elevation. But about 4500 B. C. the upper portion of the mountain caved in, leaving the caldera now filled by Crater Lake, one of the scenic jewels of the American West.

The Cascades are not the only big mountains in Oregon. The Wallowas in the northeastern corner of the state are rugged granite mountains which reach 9839 feet in Sacajawea Peak. This peak can be climbed in one long day or two days from Wallowa State Park. A trail goes up the West Fork of the Wallowa River to Adams Creek, then up the latter to Ice Lake; from there one climbs to the divide between 9832-foot Matterhorn and Sacajawea, and finally up the south ridge to the summit.

The Oregon Mountains are covered in detail in *A Climber's Guide to Oregon,* by Nicholas A. Dodge.

▲ WASHINGTON ▲

Volcanoes

Outside of Alaska, the most majestic single mountain in the U. S. is certainly Washington's Mt. Rainier. This volcanic 14,410-foot giant of the Cascade Range rises 8000 feet above its immediate neighbors and is tremendously imposing even when seen from Seattle, over 50 miles away. With 28 glaciers totaling 48-square miles of ice, Mt. Rainier has the largest glacial system in the country outside of Alaska. The Emmons Glacier, six miles long and one and seven-tenths miles wide, is the largest. The first ascent to the highest point of Rainier was that of Gen. H. Stevens and P. B. Van Trump in 1870.

There are many routes up Mt. Rainier, but the most frequently climbed is the Ingraham Glacier route, a two-day ascent from Paradise on the south side of the mountain at 5000 feet. (This route has replaced the Gibraltar Route as the standard guided "tourist" climb.) On the first day one walks three-and-a-half miles to Camp Muir (10,000 feet), where there are a couple of stone shelters. Parties usually climb from Camp Muir to the summit and return to Paradise on the second day. From Camp Muir one crosses the Cowlitz Glacier to a notch at about 10,200 feet in the Cathedral Rocks ridge, which is crossed to reach the Ingraham Glacier. Early in the summer, if crevasses are not too bad, the glacier can be climbed right up the middle; if this is impossible, it is necessary to angle to the right and ascend the rock ridge called Disappointment Cleaver. From the top of this ridge (12,300 feet) the route is via the upper Ingraham and Emmons glaciers to the summit.

Another not too difficult and frequently ascended route is via Emmons Glacier, also a two-day climb. This route begins at the White River Campground at 4500 feet on the northeast side of the mountain. Although the Ingraham and Emmons routes are not technically difficult, the fact that both routes cross heavily crevassed glaciers means that inexperienced climbers must be with a leader of proven competence. In fact, Mt. Rainier National Park regulations strictly control permission for climbing the mountain by any route, and climbers must show that they have the proper equipment and necessary experience in order to obtain this permission; the Park requires that climbers wear hard hats. For a climber or strong hiker who wants to climb Mt. Rainier,

MAP 13.   MT. RAINIER, WASHINGTON

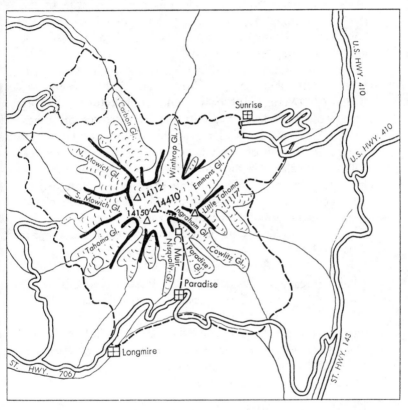

Scale 0   1   2   3   4   5   mi.

but who is not experienced on snow and ice, the best thing to do is to enroll in a one-day climbing course run by the the Mt. Rainier Guide Service; and then, provided the guides feel he can make it, the novice can join a professionally guided climbing party.

The five highest mountains in Washington are all volcanoes. After Rainier come Mt. Adams (12,307 feet), Mt. Baker (10,778 feet), Glacier Peak (10,541 feet), and Mt. St. Helens (9677 feet). Mt. Adams is a one-day climb up an easy uncrevassed snow slope on the south side. The climb begins at the end of the road past Cold Springs Camp, at 6500 feet. Adams is the easiest and safest of Washington's high volcanoes. Crampons and ice axe are useful, but rope is not needed on the regular route. Mt. Baker has a glacier system second only to Mt. Rainier's—31-square miles of ice. From the end of a logging road which turns off the Mt. Baker Highway at Glacier, the climb can be made in one long day or two days. The route is up the Coleman Glacier, which is heavily crevassed. Glacier Peak can be climbed in two days from the end of the road up the White Chuck River; the route is by way of Kennedy Hot Springs, Sitkum Creek, and Sitkum Glacier. The north slope of Fuji-like Mt. St. Helens provides a fairly easy one-day snow climb. However, rope, ice axe, and crampons are needed.

Northern Cascades

The northern half of the Cascade Mountains of Washington, from Snoqualmie Pass on U. S. Highway 10 to the Canadian border, is one of the most magnificent concentrations of mountains in the U.S. The whole vast area is a paradise for climbers, hikers, and wilderness lovers. The term "North Cascades" is generally used in a more restricted sense for that portion of the range which is north of Glacier Peak; here is a superb region of jagged peaks and glaciers that is the most alpine in the U.S. outside of Alaska. Much of the more spectacular scenery in this regon is included in North Cascades National Park, which was established in 1968. Other fine sections have also been preserved in the Ross Lake and Lake Chelan National Recreation areas, and the Pasayten and Glacier Peak Wilderness areas.

The two highest summits in the northern Cascades are the volcanoes Mt. Baker and Glacier Peak. Aside from them, the highest summits are in the following sections: 1. Wenatchee Range, west of Wenatchee; the highest is Mt. Stuart (9415 feet), a fairly easy climb. 2. The Entiat and Chelan ranges, between Glacier Peak and Lake Chelan; highest summits are Bonanza Peak (9511 feet), Mt. Fernow (9249 feet), Mt. Maude (9082 feet), and Seven Fingered Jack (9077 feet); being east of the main range crest, these peaks are less heavily glaciated than those farther west. Seven Fingered Jack and Mt. Maude are among the easier northern Cascade peaks over 9000 feet. Bonanza Peak, the highest non-volcanic mountain in the state, is a fairly difficult snow climb in early summer, and a moderate rock climb late in the season. 3. Suiattle-Agnes group, from Glacier Peak north to Cascade Pass; these are rugged and spectacular mountains with some large glaciers; highest summit is Dome Peak (8860 feet). 4. Methow Range, just east of Lake Chelan; highest peaks are North Gardner Mountain (8956 feet), Silver Star Mountain (8876 feet), and Oval Peak (8800 feet); there are few glaciers and the peaks are generally not difficult to climb. 5. Cascade Pass group, northwest of northern end of Lake Chelan; these are some of the most alpine mountains in the state; highest summits are Forbidden Peak (8815 feet), Eldorado Peak (8868 feet), and Boston Peak (8894 feet); the major peaks in this group all require technical experience. 6. Park Creek Pass–Rainy Pass group, just east of Cascade Pass group, contains some of the highest summits in the northern Cascades in Goode Mtn. (9200 feet), Buckner Mtn. (9112 feet), and Mt. Logan (9087 feet); being farther east than the Cascade Pass group they are less glaciated; also, they are easier to climb, though they do require rope. 7. Mt. Baker region; in addition to Mt. Baker, there is nearby Mt. Shuksan (9127 feet), a magnificent mountain with precipitous rock walls and hanging glaciers. 8. Picket Range, between Mt. Shuksan and Ross Lake; though they reach only 8292 feet in Mt. Fury, these are perhaps the steepest, wildest, and most spectacular group of mountains in the entire Cascades. 9. Chilliwack group, north of the Picket Range; highest are 8956-foot Mt. Redoubt and 8894-foot Mt. Spickard; this is another group of rugged and alpine mountains. 10. Ross Lake group, south and east of Ross Lake; they reach 8928 feet in Jack Mountain. 11. Pasayten-Okanogan group; located between the Pasayten and Okanogan rivers, east of Ross Lake; many summits are over 8000 feet, of which the highest is 8666-foot Mt. Lago; relatively little moisture from the Pacific reaches this far east of the Cascade crest, so there are virtually no glaciers in this large region of high, but gentle and easily ascended mountains; this is good country for hiking and horseback riding. Aside from the high peaks listed above plus many other very alpine mountains that are only slightly lower, the northern Cascades possess an inexhaustible supply of peaks, pinnacles, and walls for rock climbers.

Olympic Mountains

The Olympic Mountains receive as much as 200 feet of snowfall in a winter, and this is enough, despite the relatively low elevation of the mountains, to feed some large glaciers. The snowline is about 6000 feet elevation, the lowest in the contiguous U.S.A. and some glaciers extend to as low as 4000 feet. Below a timberline at approximately 4500 feet, the western slope of the Olympics is covered with the densest rain forests in the U. S. The east side of the Olympics is in the rain shadow, and the vegetation, glaciation, and weather are all markedly different.

The usual starting point for climbing the highest peak in the Olympics, 7954-foot Mt. Olympus, is the Hoh Ranger Station near the western edge of Olympic National Park. A 16.6-mile trail leads to Glacier Meadows (4500 feet), from where the route is by way of the Blue Glacier and the Snow Dome to the 200-foot-high summit pinnacle. Rope is needed both on the glacier and on the summit pinnacle, which late in the summer requires about 200 feet of moderate rock climbing.

Olympic is a good park for wilderness backpacking since there is an extensive trail network. The big problem is the weather, but this is ameliorated by the existence of a number of shelters along the trails.

The Washington Cascades are described in comprehensive detail in Fred Beckey's *Cascade Alpine Guide,* vols. I and II, with vol. III in process. The Olympics are described in *Climber's Guide to the Olympic Mountains.* These books, as well as several hiking guides to the areas, are all published by The Mountaineers. Seattle.

▲ ALASKA ▲

Alaska Range

By any standards Mt. McKinley is one of the greatest of mountains. Its 20,320-foot elevation makes it the highest outside of the Himalayas and the Andes, but more important is the fact that it soars a full 17,000 feet above the plains at its base; this is the greatest base-to-summit rise of any mountain on earth. By comparison Kilimanjaro floats some 14,000 feet above the African savannah, while Everest climbs 13,000 feet above the Rongbuk Monastery at the edge of the Tibetan Plateau. McKinley also claims the world's greatest rise above the treeline, which is at about 3000 feet in the region.

Mt. McKinley has two summits, the South Peak (20,320 feet) and the North Peak (19,470 feet), which are two-and-a-half miles apart. The South Peak was first climbed in 1913 by

Archdeacon Hudson Stuck, Henry Karstens, Walter Harper, and Robert Tatum. This was a fine achievement for that date, but the conquest of the North Peak three years earlier was even more noteworthy, and ranks as one of the most astonishing ventures in the history of mountaineering. A group of "sourdoughs" with no previous climbing experience, financed by a few Fairbanks businessmen and saloon keepers, set out for the mountain in midwinter. Finally in late March they found themselves encamped high on the Muldrow Glacier at 11,000 feet. After waiting a few days for good weather they continued toward the summit, which amazingly they reached in one day. The sourdoughs chose to climb the North Peak rather than the higher South Peak, presumably because it is nearer Fairbanks and they hoped that the flag they planted on the summit could be seen from the town with a telescope. For their flag they lugged a 14-foot-long flagpole all the way from the lowlands to the summit of the North Peak, but whether or not anyone was able to observe the flag from Fairbanks is not known,

The easiest route up Mt. McKinley is probably by way of the West Buttress from the Kahiltna Glacier. The route is not considered technically difficult for experienced climbers, and by hiring a plane to land climbers and equipment high on the glacier, parties can make the ascent in weeks rather than months formerly required. (Because of National Park regulations, however, airplanes cannot land inside the Park boundaries; therefore, parties usually land on the Kahiltna Glacier just outside the boundary.) Despite the relative technical ease of the West Buttress route, climbers must remember that Mt. McKinley's most formidable obstacle is the weather, and even the most experienced and best-equipped party can be thwarted by an arctic storm high on the mountain. The best weather and climbing conditions are usually in April, May, and July. The headquarters of Mt. McKinley National Park can provide pamphlets giving adminstrative requirements for climbing McKinley as well as valuable information about the climb itself.

Since the normal route up McKinley has become almost routine for the experts, there has been a search for newer and more challenging routes, of which McKinley offers a great number. Climbers have even worked their way up the 14,000-foot-high north face—the Wickersham Wall—which is certainly one of the world's highest unbroken mountain slopes; its average angle is something less than 40°. The shorter (8000 feet in one sweep) but steeper south face has also been conquered.

Mt. McKinley is the dominant peak in the Alaska Range, but the range also has many other magnificent mountains, of which the next in height are Mt. Foraker (17,400 feet) and Mt. Hunter (14,570 feet). Although in the United States Foraker is exceeded in height by only Mt. McKinley and Mt. St. Elias, it was not climbed until 1934. The ascent is technically more difficult than the easier routes on McKinley.

When seen from a distance, Mt. Hunter's contours appear rounded, and the mountain seems small beside neighboring Mt. McKinley; but Hunter is a difficult and treacherous mountain which was not climbed until 1954 (by Fred Beckey, Heinrich Harrer, and Henry Meybohm). The climb has only been repeated a few times. According to Bradford Washburn, writing in the 1968 *American Alpine Journal,* the tremendous southeast cirque of the south peak of Hunter will provide perhaps the greatest rock climbing challenge in the Mt. McKinley area.

Two other peaks in the vicinity of Mt. McKinley deserve special mention: arrowhead-shaped Mt. Huntington (12,240 feet), which is one of the most spectacular rock and ice peaks in Alaska; and Mooses Tooth (10,335 feet), a sharp rock peak. Both peaks were first climbed in 1964, Huntington by the French and Mooses Tooth by the Germans.

The Alaska Range contains much more than just Mt. McKinley and its immediate neighbors. A little over 100 miles to the east is the range's second highest group, which is topped by 13,832-foot Mt. Hayes. Even more spectacular is 12,339-foot Mt. Deborah, which Fred Beckey described as "the most sensational ice climb anyone of us had ever undertaken" (*American Alpine Journal,* 1955), after his first ascent with Harrer and Meybohm. About 75 miles east of the Mt. Hayes group, another important but rarely visited uplift reaches about 10,350 feet in Mt. Kimball.

In the southwestern part of the Alaska Range there are two groups of very impressive rock peaks which were unclimbed and virtually unknown until the 1960's. The Cathedral Spires (or Kichatna Spires) are perhaps the closest thing in North America to the rock spires of Patagonia. They are located about 40 miles southwest of the boundary of Mt. McKinley National Park. The highest, Kichatna Spire (8985 feet), was first climbed in 1966. Some 70 miles southwest of the Cathedral Spires are the Revelation Mountains, which reach 9828 feet. These mountains, which were first visited in 1967, are described by David. S. Roberts (*American Alpine Journal,* 1968) as being somewhat less sharp, but with greater vertical relief, than the Cathedral Spires. Roberts says they are so remote that they may not be visible from any inhabited land.

Coast Mountains

The Alaskan section of the Coast Mountains is shared with Canada, and is a continuation of the Coast Mountains of British Columbia. The most impressive mountains in this region are east of Petersburg, where one finds Kates Needle (10,002 feet) and Devils Thumb (9077 feet), two extremely steep and spectacular peaks. Kates Needle rises in breathtaking steepness from the valley of the Stikine River, which is just east of the peak at an altitude scarcely above sea level. However, the highest peak in this region is Mt. Ratz (10,290 feet), which is on the British Columbia side of the border.

Fairweather Range

From Cross Sound northwestward for 200 miles are the most impressive coastal mountains on earth, though they are not quite as high as the Sierra Nevada de Santa Marta of Colombia. The southern part of this section is the Fairweather Range, dominated by the 15,300-foot border peak Mt. Fairweather, whose summit is only 14 miles from the ocean; the peak was first ascended by Allen Carpé and Terris Moore in 1932. Just south of Fairweather is Mt. Crillon (12,726 feet), a peak only some 12 miles from the shores of Lituya Bay.

St. Elias Mountains

North of the Fairweather Range are the St. Elias Mountains, which are the most tremendous mountain uplift in North America, though exceeded in height by Mt. McKinley. The highest summit in the St. Elias Mountains, Mt. Logan (19,850 feet), is in Canada, and the highest Alaskan point in the range is the border peak Mt. St. Elias (18,008 feet). The summit of this superb mountain is only 20 miles from the waters of Icy Bay.

There is no technically easy route up Mt. St. Elias, which is probably the most difficult mountain over 16,000 feet in North America. Mt. St. Elias was first climbed in 1897 by the Duke of Abruzzi's Italian expedition, but the mountain was not climbed again until 1946.

The St. Elias Mountains have four other peaks over 14,000 feet which are shared by Alaska and Canada: Mt. Vancouver (15,825 feet; actually, there are several summits, the highest of which is in Canada, and the border peak is about 150 feet lower); Mt. Hubbard (15,015 feet); Mt. Alverstone (14,516 feet), and Mt. Augusta (14,070 feet). The St. Elias Mountains have some of the greatest glaciers on earth outside of the polar regions, and are primarily of interest to snow and ice climbers. However, Washburn's 1968 article in the *American Alpine Journal* lists the great west faces of Hubbard and Alverstone as offering potential routes to challenge the best of rock climbers.

Aside from the border peaks named above, the major portion of the St. Elias Mountains lies within the Yukon Territory. However, the final uplift of the range in the northwest is wholly within Alaska, and reaches about 16,550 feet in Mt. Bona, first climbed in 1930. Other high summits are Mt. Churchill (15,638 feet; this peak is just north of Bona, to which it is connected by a saddle with a 1200-foot drop); University Peak (14,470 feet; also a neighbor of Bona), and Mt. Bear (14,831 feet).

Wrangell Mountains

Northwest of the Bona region are the Wrangell Mountains, the third highest Alaskan range. Here are found the technically easiest high mountains in Alaska. In fact, airplanes have landed on or near the summits of 16,237-foot Mt. Sanford and 14,163-foot Mt. Wrangell, both of which are huge snow domes of volcanic origin. Sanford was first climbed in 1938 by Washburn and Moore, largely on skis. Wrangell was first climbed in 1908, although the party probably did not reach the very highest point. Wrangell's summit has been used by the U. S. Army and others for high altitude research, and they constructed a hut which was (maybe is) warmed by a natural heat vent from a still-steaming fumarole.

The highest summit in the Wrangell Mountains is the massive 16,390-foot Mt. Blackburn, whose 16,286-foot southeastern summit was first climbed in 1912 by Miss Dora Keen and G. W. Handy. The true summit, one-and-a-half miles to the northwest, was first climbed in 1958. One route on Blackburn is also relatively easy technically, and skis have been used much of the way.

Although the three highest Wrangell peaks can be described as relatively easy, this is only true if airplanes are used to fly over the approach difficulties—namely trailless, tangled forest, and mosquito-infested, marshy tundra—allowing parties to start out from glaciers well up the mountainsides. Here, as throughout Alaska, the airplane has made climbing possible for those with only a few weeks at their disposal. There are several bush pilots who specialize in glacier landings, and in the mountaineer's Alaska today, almost all major climbs begin from a glacier airstrip. Despite the relative technical ease with which some of the Wrangell summits can be reached, climbers cannot forget that they must still be prepared for treacherous arctic weather and be fully proficient in snow and ice climbing.

Chugach Mountains

West of the St. Elias Mountains, the coastal range is known as the Chugach Mountains, which reach 13,176 feet in Mt. Marcus Baker, first climbed by a Washburn party in 1938. In the western Chugach, just east of Anchorage, are a group of mountains reaching to 8005 feet, which since World War II have seen the closest thing in Alaska to the weekend mountaineering characteristic of the American West.

Aleutian Range

The great chain of volcanoes that extends from just west of Cook Inlet all the way to the Aleutian Islands is called the Aleutian Range. The highest summits are in the north, in the Tordrillo Mountains, where Mt. Torbert reaches 11,413 feet. To the south of the Tordrillo Mountains are the Chigmit Mountains, with Mt. Redoubt (10,197 feet) and Mt. Iliamna

(10,016 feet). The most famous mountains in the range are Mt. Katmai (6715 feet), whose eruption in 1912 was one of the greatest ever recorded, and 9387-foot Mt. Shishaldin on Unimak Island; Shishaldin is noted for the perfect symmetry of its cone.

Brooks Range

In the far north the Brooks Range extends clear across the breadth of Arctic Alaska. Much of the range consists of tundra-covered hills but there are many rugged mountains and some glaciers, particularly in the eastern part. The highest mountain in the Brooks Range is Mt. Isto (9060 feet), about 100 miles from the Yukon border. One group of very startling granite pinnacles is the Arrigetch Peaks, located northwest of Bettles.

Further Sources of Information
on Climbing and Hiking in Alaska

Alaska is one of the great mountaineering frontiers of the world, but it should be made quite clear that the high mountains of the state are no place for inexperienced climbers. Even hiking in the Alaska wilderness requires careful preparation. A pamphlet entitled *Hiking the McKinley Back Country,* available from Mount McKinley National Park, gives a good outline of what is needed.

▲ HAWAII ▲

If the rise from base to summit is taken as the standard of height for mountains, then the Hawaiian volcanoes Mauna Kea (13,796 feet) and Mauna Loa (13,680 feet) are nearly 32,000 feet high, since they rise from a base 18,000 feet below the level of the sea. Thus in a sense they are the highest mountains on earth. Even if we ignore the lower 18,000 feet, massive, gently sloping Mauna Loa is probably still the largest single mountain on earth in terms of bulk. In fact, between them Mauna Kea and Mauna Loa cover nearly half the total territory of the state of Hawaii. The two mountains are called "shield" volcanoes, which means they were built up gradually by lava flowing from a number of vents, rather than through the deposition of material ejected explosively from a single, central pipe, as in the case of symmetrical "composite" cones like Mt. Fuji.

Mauna Kea has a four-wheel-drive vehicle road to its summit. (However, as of 1968 the public was not generally allowed to use it; incidentally, a summit observatory was under construction at that time.) Hikers can start at Kilohana (9620 feet) in the Hale Pohaku Area, which is reached by a turnoff from the road across the 7000-foot saddle between Mauna Kea and Mauna Loa. The distance to the summit is about six miles, and the average hiker can cover it in five hours. Mauna Kea ("White Mountain") receives more snow than Mauna Loa and near the summit in winter there are accumulations suitable for diehard skiers; there has even been talk of installing a ski lift. Winter snows reach down to about 10,000 feet.

The trail to the summit of Mauna Loa begins at the end of the Mauna Loa Strip Road, at 6662 feet elevation on the east side of the mountain. The trail is 18 miles one-way and the round trip ordinarily requires three days. There are huts at 10,000 feet (seven miles up the trail) and at the summit crater at 13,250 feet. Mauna Loa can be climbed on horseback; as on Mauna Kea there is an administrative jeep road to the top, but it is usually closed.

The Hawaiian Volcanoes National Park, which includes Mauna Loa but not Mauna Kea, is one of the most interesting and accessible exhibits of volcanism on earth. Mauna Loa itself is rarely active, but Kilauea Crater—at 4000 feet elevation on the east slope of Mauna Loa—has erupted about once a year in recent years. In 1959, in one of the greatest spectacles ever put on by nature, Kilauea shot fountains of molten lava 1900 feet into the air.

Another massive shield volcano, 10,023-foot Haleakala, covers most of the island of Maui. The unique volcanic desert of its huge summit area has been set aside as Haleakala National Park. Haleakala's summit is reached by road.

Mt. Waialeale (5080 feet) on Kauai comes far down on a list of high peaks, but its top leads the world in recorded rainfall with an average of 468 inches a year—even more than Cherrapunji in the Indian state of Assam, which claimed the record until recently.

MAP 14.   MAUNA KEA and MAUNA LOA, HAWAII

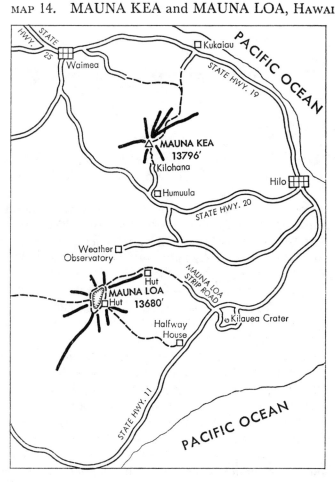

Scale 0 2 4 6 8 10 12 mi.

▲ WESTERN CANADA ▲

St. Elias Mountains

There are two main mountain systems in western Canada, the coastal system and the Rocky Mountains. The highest summits are in the northern portion of the coastal system, in the St. Elias Mountains (and their southern extension, the Fairweather Range). Here Mt. Logan rears its massive crest to 19,850 feet, second only to Mt. McKinley in North America, and here are all of Canada's other peaks over 14,000 feet, including Mt. St. Elias (18,008 feet; on the border with Alaska), Mt. Lucania (17,147 feet), Kings Peak (17,130 feet), Mt. Steele (16,440 feet), Mt. Wood (15,885 feet), Mt. Vancouver (15,825 feet; on the border), Mt. Slaggard (15,575 feet), Mt. McCauley (15,475 feet), Mt. Fairweather (15,300 feet; on the border), Mt. Hubbard (15,015 feet; on the border), Mt. Walsh (14,780 feet), Mt. Alverstone (14,516 feet; on the border), Mt. McArthur (14,500 feet), and Mt. Augusta (14,070 feet; on the border).

In pre-airplane days the St. Elias Mountains were extremely difficult of access and weeks were required just to reach the high peaks. Now experienced pilots can land climbers and their equipment high on the glaciers, and it is possible to climb one of the major summits within the time limits of an average vacation. However, climbing in the St. Elias Mountains still requires a full-scale expedition equipped and trained to handle some of the most severe mountain weather.

Coast Mountains

South and east of the St. Elias Mountains are the Coast Mountains which extend all the way to the Washington border. The northern part of the Coast Mountains is located along the border between the Alaska panhandle and British Columbia, and contains some very impressive peaks, the highest of which is Mt. Ratz (10,290 feet; located on the Canadian side of the border). But the highest summits in the Coast Mountains are farther south, in the Mt. Waddington region. The magnificent 13,177-foot Mt. Waddington itself is the highest peak in Canada outside of the St. Elias and Fairweather ranges. Though it is only 175 miles from Vancouver, the peak is in an extremely remote region and was not ascended until 1936, after several unsuccessful attempts. Fortunately for today's climbers, float planes can now take parties to Ghost Lake, east of Waddington at 3800 feet, and the ascent can be made in about 10 days from there. There is no technically easy route up Waddington, and even the easiest, via the southeast face, involves Class 4 and 5 climbing.

Other noteworthy peaks in the neighborhood of Waddington are 12,559-foot Mt. Tiedemann, the second highest summit in the range, and the Serra Peaks, a group of steep rock towers reaching 12,000 feet. The Waddington region has the most extensive glaciers in the range south of Alaska, and one of them reaches down to 700 feet above sea level.

Outside of the Waddington group the highest peak in the Coast Mountains is 11,590-foot Monarch Mount, southeast of Bella Coola. Although the greater portion of the Coast Mountains remains quite remote, airplanes and logging roads have in recent years made a number of areas accessible for the first time. For climbers who just want a brief introduction to the range, the most accessible major peak is 8787-foot Mt. Garibaldi, some 40 miles north of Vancouver. From the Diamond Head Chalet, reached by road, the climb can be made in one day. The Coast Mountains south of the Alaska panhandle are covered in Dick Culbert's *A Climber's Guide to the Coastal Ranges of British Columbia.*

Rocky Mountains

The term "Canadian Rockies" is generally used to denote only the portion of the Rocky Mountain system between the U. S. border and central British Columbia; however, the system itself extends farther north and includes the Mac-Kenzie and Selwyn mountains along the Yukon-Northwest Territories border, as well as other lesser ranges. The best known section of the Canadian Rockies is in Banff and Jasper National parks, along the Alberta-British Columbia border. The Banff-Jasper highway, which is east of and parallel to the crestline, provides one of the longest continuous panoramas of mountain magnificence that auto-bound tourists are ever likely to find. For mountaineers with limited time, there are interesting and challenging major-peak climbs very close to the highway, including Mt. Victoria (11,365 feet) and Mt. Athabasca (11,452 feet).

The main portion of the Canadian Rockies is an elongated, almost straight uplift of markedly stratified sedimentary or metamorphosed rocks. Because the rock is loose and dangerous, the mountains are less favored by rock climbers than by snow and ice climbers. The highest peak is 12,972-foot Mt. Robson in British Columbia's Mt. Robson Provincial Park, which adjoins Jasper National Park. Robson, which rises 10,000 precipitous feet above its immediate base, is without doubt the most majestic and dominating peak in the Canadian Rockies, as well as the highest. It is also one of the most difficult to climb, and its ascent requires a high degree of climbing skill on a mountain notorious for its bad weather; only thoroughly experienced climbers should consider it. Access to the immediate base of Mt. Robson is easy, requiring only one day from the Mount Robson station on the railway between Edmonton and Prince George. From the station the climb would take about four days round trip in the unlikely event that the weather was perfect; it would be more prudent to allow ten days. Routes on Robson as well as all other major peaks in the Canadian Rockies are described in *Climber's Guide to the Rocky Mountains of Canada* (2 vols.), by Putnam, Boles, Jones and Kruszyna.

There are a number of high peaks in the Canadian Rockies which offer routes suitable for climbers of moderate experience, provided they are with a qualified leader. Among them are the third highest, 12,085-foot North Twin, and the sixth highest, 11,870-foot Mt. Assiniboine. The latter, a very steep, Matterhorn-like pyramid, is one of the most spectacular peaks in the Rockies, but like the Swiss Matterhorn it is considerably easier than it looks. About five days should be allowed for an ascent of Assiniboine. For hikers and climbers with limited ambitions, scrambles in the 7000- to 8000-foot range are not difficult to find. In recent years expert climbers, in their unceasing search for newer and greater challenges, have successfully assaulted a number of the tremendous, previously untouched 3000- to 4000-foot-high north or east walls of peaks in the Canadian Rockies, including those of Mt. Temple, Mt. Assiniboine, Mt. Edith Cavell, Mt. Chephren, and the peaks of the Ramparts group.

The most impressive mountains in the Rocky Mountain system north of Mt. Robson are the Logan Mountains, which are part of the Selwyn Mountains. Here are found some of the most spectacular granite peaks on the continent. Particularly startling in appearance is Proboscis Peak, a sharp blade of rock with an almost perpendicular 2000-foot-high east face and a west face only slightly lower. Timberline in the Rocky Mountains of Canada decreases from 7500 feet near the U. S. border, to 6000 feet at Mt. Robson, and 3500 feet in the Selwyn Mountains.

Interior Ranges of British Columbia

To the west of the Canadian Rockies is a long, straight valley, the Rocky Mountain Trench, which separates the Rockies from what are called the Interior Ranges of British Columbia. These ranges are the Cariboo, Monashee, Selkirk, and Purcell mountains. The highest summits of each of these ranges are Mt. Sir Wilfred Laurier (11,250 feet) in the Cariboos, Mt. Monashee (10,650 feet) in the Monashees, Mt. Sir Sandford (11,590 feet) in the Selkirks, and Mt.

Farnham (11,342 feet) in the Purcells. There is good climbing and wilderness exploration to be found in all four ranges, but the most impressive and most accessible peaks are in the Purcells and Selkirks. The Bugaboo group in the Purcells is one of the most spectacular and popular alpine playgrounds on the continent. Boulder Camp, the usual climbing base for these quite accessible mountains, is only a half-day trek from the end of a road which turns off Highway 95 just south of Spillimacheen. The Bugaboos reach 11,150 feet in Howser Spire. The most accessible peaks in the Selkirks are those which rise above Rogers Pass on the Trans-Canada Highway. Mt. Sir Donald (10,818 feet), a superb pyramidal peak, is one of several that can be climbed in one day from the road. All four of the Interior Ranges are covered in *Climber's Guide to the Interior Ranges of British Columbia—North,* by Putnam, and *Climber's Guide to the Interior Ranges of British Columbia—South,* by Putnam and Kruszyna.

▲ MEXICO ▲

For American climbers who want to warm up for the Himalayas or the Andes, or just to have a try at climbing mountains several thousand feet higher than the Rockies and the Sierra Nevada, the great volcanoes of Mexico are the obvious place to go. The highest is 18,700-foot Orizaba, which is exceeded in height in North America by only Mt. McKinley and Mt. Logan; the peak's Aztec name—Citlaltepetl ("star mountain")—is now favored by many Mexicans. Mexico City's backyard giants, 17,887-foot Popocatepetl and 17,343-foot Ixtaccihuatl, rank fifth and seventh in North America. Popocatepetl, which means "smoking mountain" in Aztec, is called "Popo" for short, and Ixtaccihuatl (meaning "sleeping woman") is nicknamed "Ixty."

Orizaba is a symmetrical cone which can be seen on a clear day from far out in the Gulf of Mexico. The mountain, which last erupted in 1566, was first climbed by F. Maynard and G. Reynolds in 1848. The base for the usual route up Orizaba is the small town of Tlachichuca, which can be reached by bus or car in half a day from Mexico City, by way of Puebla. From Tlachichuca a jeep road leads to the Piedra Grande Hut (14,400 feet), some 1000 feet above timberline on Orizaba's north slope. Arrangements for jeep transport and guides can be made at Tlachichuca's largest store, which is operated by the Reyes family. From the Piedra Grande Hut climbers generally reach the summit and return in one day. On the easiest route, which goes almost directly from the hut to the summit, only crampons and ice axe are needed, but routes requiring rope can also be found on the north and east sides of Orizaba. During holidays, especially Christmas, the Piedra Grande Hut may be full, so climbers should be prepared to sleep out.

Popo is better known than Orizaba because its Fuji-like cone is easily visible from Mexico City, just 45 miles away. The normal route up Popo is the Las Cruces route, which begins at Tlamacas (13,000 feet), at the Popo end of the

MAP 15.   POPOCATEPETL and IXTACCIHUATL, Mexico

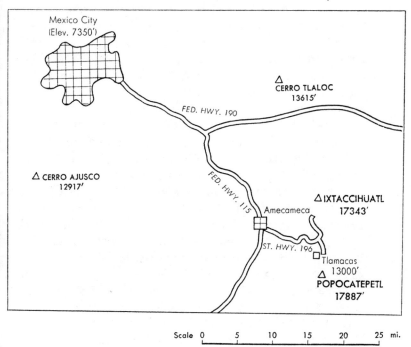

Mexico City
(Elev. 7350')

△ CERRO TLALOC
13615'

FED. HWY. 190

△ CERRO AJUSCO
12917'

FED. HWY. 115

△IXTACCIHUATL
17343'

Amecameca

ST. HWY. 196

Tlamacas
13000'

△ POPOCATEPETL
17887'

Scale   0   5   10   15   20   25   mi.

saddle between Popo and Ixty. Tlamacas, where there is a hotel and parking lot, can be reached by car from Mexico City in a little over an hour, by way of Amecameca. Although the Las Cruces route is easy, much of the way is over snow, and crampons and ice axe are useful. The route goes straight up to the low point on the crater, at about 17,000 feet, then counterclockwise to the highest point. The vertical walls of Popo's extremely impressive crater are over 600 feet high at the lowest point on the rim and 1500 feet high just below the summit. Popo's last major eruption was in 1802.

Popo's highest point was probably reached for the first time in 1827, by Glennie and Taylor, but the most notable early climbs on the mountain were led by two of Cortez's men, Diego Ordaz in 1519, and Francisco Montano in 1521. The primary motive seems to have been to obtain sulphur for making gunpowder, though William H. Prescott, in his classic *History of the Conquest of Mexico,* suggests that another motive was to demonstrate the Spaniards' prowess to the Aztecs, who had a great fear of the "Smoking Mountain." Though Popo's crater has been estimated to hold thousands of tons of sulphur, Cortez's men were too exhausted to do much useful mining. In his official report to the King, Cortez reflected that "it would be less inconvenient, on the whole, to import . . . powder from Spain."

Ixty, though also volcanic in origin, is a long three-humped ridge rather than a cone; no semblance of a crater remains. It was first climbed in 1889 by James de Salis, a Swiss. Ixty is the most difficult to climb of Mexico's three great volcanoes. Step-cutting may be required, there is some exposure on the ridge, and route-finding problems are greater than on Popo or Orizaba; rope should be taken. The starting point for the normal route up Ixty is also on the Popo-Ixty saddle, the low point of which is about 12,000 feet. The climb can be done in one very long day or in two days, spending the night at one of several huts on the mountain, for instance the Knees Hut (knees of the Sleeping Woman, that is).

Although Orizaba, Popo, and Ixty get most of the attention, they are not the only high mountains in Mexico. Other major volcanoes include 15,016-foot Nevado de Toluca, 50 miles southwest of Mexico City (there is an automobile road almost to the summit); Malinche (14,636 feet), halfway between Popo and Orizaba; Nauhcampatepetl (14,084 feet), north of Orizaba; and Nevado de Colima (13,993 feet), due west of Mexico City and about 60 miles from the Pacific coast.

Along the Pacific coast the Sierra Madre Occidental in the north and the Sierra Madre del Sur in the south extend almost the length of Mexico. There are few peaks over 10,000 feet, but there are unlimited opportunities for mountain and canyon exploration. Some of the canyons, called *barrancos,* rival those of the Colorado River. The ranges of Baja California culminate 100 miles south of the border in the Sierra de San Pedro Martir, where Picacho del Diablo, a rugged granite mountain, reaches 10,100 feet. The ascent is a rock scramble. The favorite rock-climbing areas of Mexico City climbers are the Window Rocks and Bishop Rock, both in Hidalgo State, just north of Mexico City.

The best time for climbing the high mountains of Mexico is the dry season, November through April. Guides for either the high peaks or rock climbing near Mexico City can be hired through the Mexican Guide School. Reforma #76, Desp. 1707, Mexico, D. F. The school can also provide additional climbing information.

▲ CENTRAL AMERICA ▲

Some people mistakenly think that the string of seven tropical countries that make up Central America have nothing but steaming jungles. In fact, however, a good portion of the region is quite mountainous, and much of the population lives in pleasant temperate highlands.

The highest mountains in Central America are those of Guatemala, which claims 13 volcanoes over 3000 meters (9843 feet). First among them is 13,812-foot Tajumulco, about 12 miles east of the Mexican border. There is a trail which takes about five hours (distance: five miles) from the town of San Sebastian (about 9800 feet) to the summit of Tajumulco; guides are available in San Sebastian. Guides can also be found for most of the other high peaks, either locally or through the Federacion de Andinismo, Palacio de los Deportes, Guatemala City. After Tajumulco, the highest volcanoes in Guatemala are Tacana (13,428 feet) and Acatenango (12,992 feet). The highest nonvolcanic mountains in Central America are the Alto Cuchumatanes (which reach 13,100 feet), 100 miles northwest of Guatemala City.

Outside of Guatemala, the highest Central American peak is the 12,860-foot volcano Chirripo in Costa Rica. More famous is 11,260-foot Irazu, which erupted in 1963 and 1964, and covered Costa Rica's capital city of San Jose with volcanic ash. Panama claims 11,410-foot Volcan de Chiriqui.

In Central America the dry season is from November to April, though there is also a shorter dry season in July. The upper limit of forest in the region is somewhat over 10,000 feet, and the higher slopes are grass covered.

▲ WEST INDIES ▲

There are many good reasons for vacationing in the West Indies, but mountaineering is not generally considered one of them. Nevertheless, there are a number of attractions of undoubted interest to mountain enthusiasts. The highest summits in the West Indies are on the island of Hispanola, which is split into the two countries of Haiti and the Dominican Republic. The highest single peak, 10,417-foot Pico Duarte, is in the Dominican Republic. The starting point for the trail to the summit of Duarte is Arroyo Chicharron (about 6500 feet), which is reached by road from either Constanza or Jarabacoa; guides can be procured in either of these two towns. Additional information about hiking and climbing in the Dominican Republic can be obtained from the Federacion Nacional de Alpinismo y Excursionismo Dominicano, Estadio Juan Pablo Duarte, Santo Domingo.

The Haitian mountains reach 8793 feet in the Selle Massif, southeast of Port au Prince. But the most interesting mountain scene in Haiti is the unusual 3000-foot-high square-topped peak which from Cap Haitien can be seen 20 miles to the south. Closer approach reveals that the oddly shaped summit is actually a gigantic fortress, the Citadel, built by the Haitian king Henri Cristophe early in the 19th century. This fabulous mountaintop castle is reached on horseback or on foot.

Perhaps the most spectacular mountains in the Caribbean are 2619-foot Gros Piton and 2461-foot Petit Piton, which rise sheerly from the water's edge on the island of St. Lucia. An early attempt to climb the steeper of the two, Petit Piton, is said to have ended in disaster as one by one all four English sailors in the party were bitten by the deadly fer-de-lance (pit viper).

The most notorious mountain in the West Indies is the volcano Mt. Pelée (4800 feet) on Martinique. On 8 May 1902, after a couple of weeks of intermittent eruption, a great rift opened on the side of the mountain and released a super-heated mixture of steam, poisonous gases, and pulverized rock. In minutes this incandescent cloud rolled across the town of St. Pierre, killing all but one of the 30,000 inhabitants. The lone survivor was saved only because he was locked up in a thick-walled prison awaiting execution the following day. Today, a new town of St Pierre stands once again on the same location—below the gentle, peaceful slopes of Mt. Pelée.

The highest point in Cuba is 6500-foot Turquino in the Sierra Maestra, in Oriente Province. Blue Mountain Peak (7402 feet) in the Blue Mountains of eastern Jamaica is the highest on that island.

▲ GUIANA HIGHLANDS ▲

The Guiana Highlands, which occupy the southeastern corner of Venezuela and the adjoining portions of Guyana and Brazil, are a unique region of giant mesas bordered by cliffs, some over 3000 feet high. The largest mesas are many square miles in area and perhaps should not be considered mountains at all, but with some of the highest rock walls anywhere on earth, they undoubtedly cannot but appeal to mountain enthusiasts.

The region is very thinly populated, mostly by primitive Indians, missionaries, and diamond miners, and it has just begun to welcome its first tourists. Most of it remains untrodden, and few tourists do more to disturb the wilderness than make a quick flight past Angel Falls, the world's highest. With a free fall of 2648 feet (1200 feet higher than Upper Yosemite Falls) and a total drop of 3212 feet, Angel Falls gives a good indication of the scale of these rock walls. Many other waterfalls in the region are only slightly lower. Angel

Falls plunges from the edge of Auyantepui (9688 feet), one of the highest mesas in the Guiana Highlands.

The starting point for climbing Auyantepui is a place called Guayaraca at 3600 feet, near which there is a small airstrip. The rugged climb from there to Campo Libertador on the top of the mesa takes two days. Indian guides and porters can be hired for the climb. The base of Angel Falls can be reached from the tourist camp of Canaima in about four days by outboard-powered canoes up the Carrao and Churun rivers.

Perhaps the most famous mountain in the Highlands is 9094-foot Roraima, at the point where Venezuela, Guyana, and Brazil meet. Here Conan Doyle placed his fictional "Lost World" inhabited by prehistoric monsters long extinct elsewhere.

▲ BRAZIL ▲

Brazil has some of the best-known mountain scenery in the world—right in the middle of Rio de Janeiro. Some rock climbing has been done on the granite domes for which the city is famed, but the city's potential as an urban Yosemite is limited by the tropical heat and vegetation.

The highest summits in the coastal ranges of eastern Brazil are Bandeira (9462 feet), 200 miles northeast of Rio, and 9255-foot Itatiaya, 100 miles west-northwest of Rio. Bandeira was long considered the highest in the country, but Neblina (about 3000 meters, or 9843 feet) in the Guiana Highlands near the northern tip of Brazil, was recently discovered to be higher.

▲ ARGENTINA-CHILE ▲

The highest mountain in the world outside of Central Asia is 22,835-foot Aconcagua, which lies entirely in Argentina just across the border from Chile. Aconcagua is a bulky giant which rises some 4000 feet above its neighbors and is easily visible from the Pacific on a clear day. The mountain is composed of uplifted volcanic material but is not itself a volcano.

Aconcagua has been climbed many times by the "normal route," which ends up on the northwest ridge. The final portion of the climb is up an interminably long scree slope, but there are no technical difficulties. Nevertheless, Aconcagua is definitely not a mountain to be taken lightly. The elevation is great enough to be a real problem for anyone except the best climbers in top condition. In fact, the altitude has been a greater problem than on higher peaks in the Himalayas because the relative ease of access and the lack of technical problems has allowed climbers to reach the upper slopes without taking the time necessary for gradual acclimatization. There have been a large number of fatalities on the mountain because climbers without sufficient experience or adequate equipment have been misled by the technical ease, and then been overwhelmed by the combination of altitude and severe weather. There is little letup in the gale-force winds which blow over the top of Aconcagua and keep the upper slopes swept clear of snow for a good portion of the year. Snowline in the Aconcagua region is at about 14,500 feet, but varies considerably according to local variations in precipitation. In winter there is substantial snowfall, but the summer is very dry.

The regular route up Aconcagua begins at Puente del Inca (9000 feet), which is 13 airline miles southeast of the peak and just east of the Paso de la Cumbre on the main rail and road link between Santiago and Buenos Aires. At Puente del Inca, mules can be hired for the 27-mile trip up the barren Horcones River valley to the hut on the west side of the peak at Plaza de Mulas (13,000 feet), the usual base camp. From here the trail angles upward to the northwest ridge, which leads to the summit. The trail is suitable for mules all the way to the Independencia Hut at 19,750 feet. There are also a couple of other huts along the route, including one at 21,325 feet.

In sharp contrast to the relatively gentle north slope, Aconcagua's south face is a stupendous rock and ice wall 10,000 feet high; it is probably the most gigantic precipice in the entire Andes. The wall lies straight ahead during the the approach march up the Horcones River valley.

The Swiss guide Mattias Zurbriggen, who was a member of an expedition led by E. A. Fitzgerald, made the first ascent

MAP 16. ACONCAGUA, Argentina-Chile

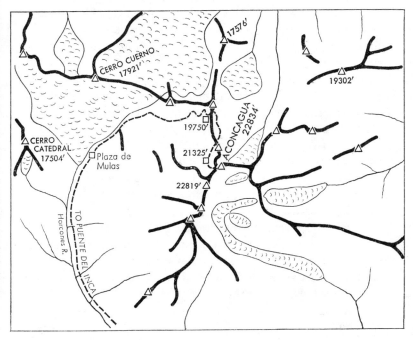

CERRO CUERNO
17921'

17576'

19302'

CERRO
CATEDRAL
17504'

19750'

ACONCAGUA
22834'

21325'

22819'

□ Plaza de
Mulas

TO PUENTE DEL INCA

Horcones R.

Scale 0   1   2 mi.

of Aconcagua alone on January 14, 1897. A month later two other expedition members, the Englishman Stuart Vines and the Italian porter Lanti, repeated the ascent. Fitzgerald himself deserves some credit too; although he was physically unable to overcome the effects of the altitude, he climbed several times to the point of utter exhaustion and ended up spending a total of 15 nights at 19,000 feet. Vines and Zurbriggen also made the first ascent of Tupungato (21,489 feet), which is on the Chile-Argentina border about 50 miles south of Aconcagua. Their climb was almost as long and grueling as Aconcagua but again they found no technical difficulties. The third giant of the Aconcagua region is Mercedario (21,885 feet), an ice-capped peak 45 miles north of Aconcagua.

North of Aconcagua for some 300 miles the Andes have one main crest which contains a number of peaks over 20,000 feet and which marks the border between Chile and Argentina. At about 28° this crest divides, and from there northward all the way to southern Peru there are two main crests. Between them is a high plateau which in height and extent is second in the world to Tibet. The Chile-Argentina portion of this plateau is called the Puna de Atacama. The floor of the Puna averages about 12,000 feet elevation and is a barren, virtually waterless desert covered by salt flats and great expanses of scree. There are some volcanic peaks in the center of the Puna, but the highest summits are concentrated along the bordering crests. The snowline in parts of the Puna rises to nearly 20,000 feet—perhaps the highest on earth—and the volcanic slopes of the peaks are generally quite gentle. Therefore even the highest peaks are technically easy, and the main problems climbers face are inaccessibility, altitude, cold, and wind. Some high and relatively easy first ascents are there for the taking. The highest summit is 22,539-foot Ojos del Salado which is the world's highest volcano (now dormant). It was first climbed in 1937 by a Polish party.

It should be mentioned that east of the main crest of this part of the Andes there is a large region of lower but still quite interesting mountains which extends far into Argentina.

In a number of cases climbers who thought they were the first to reach the summits of mountains in the Puna de Atacama, as well as some peaks north and south of the Puna, were surprised to find archaeological remains from pre-Spanish days. The highest and most extensive finds thus far are on 22,057-foot Llullaillaco. On a shoulder of the peak at 21,650 feet are the remains of a large structure which was 20 feet long, 10 feet wide, and 10 feet high, and had walls three feet thick and a wooden roof; what is left of a corral for llamas stands nearby. The presence of food grains and utensils among the ruins indicated that the structure had been occupied for extended periods. A stairway led from the large building to two small huts 100 feet below the summit. The first ascent of Llullaillaco in modern times was made by a Chilean party in 1952. On other peaks in the region, climbers have come across such interesting relics as sacrificial altars, silver idols, stone axeheads, the mummified body of a boy, and—on 20,952-foot El Toro—a 450-year-old mummified body which was still sitting in the sacrificial position and wearing the sacrificial garments. Evelio Echevarria describes these fascinating discoveries in the article "The South American Indian as

Pioneer Alpinist," in the May 1968 *Alpine Journal*. He points out that finds have been discovered so far on 16 summits over 18,000 feet, and concludes that the Indians used the mountaintops as watchtowers and/or sacrificial shrines. The ascents were made by the Quechua, Ayamara, and Atacamenan Indians, and may have begun as early as the 14th century. There has even been speculation that the Indians may have climbed or attempted to climb Aconcagua; although Aconcagua is south of the Puna de Atacama, other remains have been found on summits this far south. The only evidence that there may have been climbing high on Aconcagua was the discovery in 1950 of the frozen carcass of what was reported to be a guanaco (the undomesticated cousin of the llama) on the ridge between Aconcagua's main summit and the southwest summit. This is far above the normal range for these animals, and no explanation for the animal's presence has been made. But it is interesting to recall the discovery of a llama corral at nearly 22,000 feet on Llullaillaco. Incidentally, the carcass still rests near the top of Aconcagua, and it has yet to be thoroughly examined.

The most accessible climbing region for most Chilean mountaineers is just east of Santiago, where one finds such frequently climbed peaks as Marmolejo (20,013 feet), San Jose volcano (19,292 feet), and Cerro Plomo (17,815 feet). South of Santiago the Andes rapidly decrease in height, but not in grandeur. Between 39° and 42° latitude lies the beautiful and popular Lakes District, where the highest peak is the volcano Lanin (12,388 feet); however, the snow-capped symmetrical cone of 8728-foot Osorno is better known. Other well-known and rugged mountains in the district include

11,253-foot Tronador and 8182-foot Puntiagudo, which is an impressive spirelike peak. The Bariloche-Los Alerces section of the Lakes District of Argentina is perhaps the most popular climbing center in that country; the highest summit is Cerro Tres Picos (8530 feet). The snowline in the Lakes District is at about 5300 feet.

From the Lakes District to the Strait of Magellan is the region of Patagonia. Although in altitude this is one of the lowest portions of the Andes, it nevertheless contains some of the world's most impressive mountains. The highest peak is 12,716-foot San Valentin at $46\frac{1}{2}°$ latitude, but the truly amazing mountains are still farther south. There is of course no objective standard for selecting the most spectacular mountain on earth, but one claimant for such a distinction would certainly be Fitz Roy at $48\frac{1}{2}°$ latitude in Patagonia. Fitz Roy, which faces the Argentinian pampas to the east and the southern Patagonian icecap to the west, is a sheer-walled granite pinnacle which rises an incredible 6000 feet directly above the glaciers at its base. This legendary mountain-to-end-all-mountains was first climbed in 1952 by the Frenchmen Lionel Terray and Guido Magnone. Near Fitz Roy are several aiguilles, such as 10,263-foot Cerro Torre, which are, if anything, even more incredible looking than Fitz Roy itself, though on a slightly less grand scale. About 120 miles south of Fitz Roy is the Paine group whose sheer rock spires and near-vertical 4000-foot-high walls invite comparison with the Fitz Roy group; the highest summit in the Paine group is 10,007 feet.

The Chilean coast from 45° latitude to Cape Horn (56°) is virtually uninhabited and uninhabitable. The region is a maze of fjords, channels, and islands, and the lowlands are covered by an almost impenetrable rain forest which extends right up to the edge of the glaciers. The crest of the Patagonian Andes carries two large icecaps, the northern from $46\frac{1}{2}°$ to $47\frac{1}{2}°$ and the southern from $48°$ to $51\frac{1}{2}°$. The snowline decreases from approximately 4300 feet in northern Patagonia to 2300 feet on the island of Tierra del Fuego, but as far north as $47°$ some glaciers reach the sea. The greatest obstacle climbers and explorers face in Patagonia and Tierra del Fuego is the weather. Savage winds, accompanied by driving snow or rain, sometimes blow unabated for weeks on end. The weather is supposed to be somewhat better in winter than in summer. Tierra del Fuego's mountains rise sharply from the water's edge and reach 8760 feet in Mt. Darwin, first climbed by Eric Shipton's party in 1962.

▲ BOLIVIA ▲

The Andes of Bolivia consist of a single main range on the west, and a series of topographically more complicated ranges on the east; between them is the high plateau called the Altiplano. The highest peak in Bolivia, Nevado Sajama (21,391 feet), is one of many volcanoes that dot the crest of the western range, the Cordillera Occidental. Sajama rises directly above the Altiplano about 120 miles southwest of

La Paz, and its base can be reached in a day by bus from La Paz. The mountain can be climbed without great difficulty, although the glaciers that cover the upper slopes are crevassed and steep enough to require some step-cutting. Far more severe than the technical problems are the cold, wind, and altitude.

Sajama stands near the northern end of the Bolivian portion of the Cordillera Occidental (the range continues northward into Peru). South of Sajama the range follows the Chile-Bolivia border and contains many volcanoes which, though high, are generally easy to climb. The extreme dryness causes the snowline to rise very high here, which means that snow and ice problems are minimal on even the highest peaks. On a number of peaks of 19,000 feet or over the glaciers are small, and may even be nonexistent on the northern slopes. On the southern portion of the Chile-Bolivia border the snowline rises to approximately 19,500 feet, about as high as any place on earth.

The ranges of eastern Bolivia reach their climax in the the Cordillera Real east of La Paz. These are the most alpine and, with the exception of Nevado Sajama, the highest mountains in Bolivia. In 21,201-foot Illimani, which is just southeast of La Paz, the residents of that city can claim the highest "hometown mountain" of any major city on earth. The ascent of Illimani is steeper and involves more snow work than Sajama, but is less difficult than some of the peaks farther north, in the Sorata massif. This massif, with the most heavily glaciated peaks in the range, is located about 50 miles north of La Paz; the highest summits are 21,082-foot Ancohuma and 20,873-foot Illampu.

Just west of the Sorata massif is Lake Titicaca. At 12,500 feet elevation, this lake is the highest significant body of navigable water on earth, and it provides a unique opportunity to be simultaneously seasick and mountain sick. From Illimani south-southeastward to the Argentine border, the ranges to the east of the Altiplano contain numerous easily ascended summits between 15,000 and 18,000 feet; some of them are unclimbed. In the Cocapata range, north of the town of Cochabamba, there are fine rock peaks which reach 17,159 feet in Incachaca; Calacruz (*ca.* 5100 meters, or 16,733 feet) is described as a Matterhorn-like tower; it and several other impressive peaks were apparently unclimbed as of 1968. The highest developed ski area in the world, Chacaltaya, is just a little over an hour's drive from La Paz. A few days of skiing at 16,500 feet should do wonders for one's acclimatization.

People whose childhood dreams took them to Tibet need not feel frustrated by the political inaccessibility of that country, for the Bolivian Altiplano is a good substitute. At 12,000 feet or more elevation, the Altiplano is nearly as high as Tibet, though its area is only about one-tenth as large. Like Tibet, the Altiplano is always cool or cold, though it does not have such a severe winter; also, like Tibet, it is dry and barren, and sparsely populated by a rugged race of mountain people.

▲ PERU ▲

Peru probably has more to offer the mountaineer than any other Andean country, although its highest peak, 22,205-foot Huascaran, is exceeded in height by a number of summits in Chile and Argentina. The culmination of the Peruvian Andes is the Cordillera Blanca north of Lima. In this 120-mile-long range there are, in addition to Huascaran, about 40 other peaks over 6000 meters (19,685 feet). These are the greatest tropical mountains on earth, and because of their nearness to the Equator the snow conditions are quite different from those of mountains in the higher latitudes. Above the snowline even the steepest slopes are draped with ice, while the summits often consist of incredible overhanging cornices. These cornices have caused several prudent parties to forego the privilege of standing on the highest point of their peak. The snowline is about 15,500 feet, and the tongues of the glaciers generally extend down to about 14,500 feet.

In recent years the Cordillera Blanca has become a popular goal for expeditions from all the major climbing countries. The time and funds needed are considerably less than are required for the Himalayas, while the climbing rewards are felt by many to be nearly as great. With the steadily increasing influx of climbers, the people of the nearby villages have begun to follow in the footsteps of the 19th-century Alpine villagers, and now experienced porters and even guides for certain climbs can be found in the towns of Huaras and Yungay. Huaras, at 10,000 feet, serves as the base for the peaks in the southern part of the range, while Yungay (8500 feet), which is down the Santa River valley from Huaras, serves the more northerly peaks including Huascaran. The two towns can be reached by car in a day from Lima; there are also (as of 1968) twice-weekly flights from Lima to Caras, a few miles north of Yungay.

Most of the major peaks of the Cordillera Blanca involve technical ice climbing, and are therefore the preserve of experienced parties. Huascaran itself has been climbed many times and is not considered to be one of the more difficult peaks of the range, though climbers must be experienced in snow and ice climbing and, needless to say, well acclimatized. The normal route up Huascaran takes about six days round trip from the village of Musho (about 9850 feet), which is reached by road from Yungay. A base camp at 14,500 feet, just below the permanent snows, can be reached from Musho in one day on foot or on horseback. The route from there goes by way of the 19,500-foot saddle between Huascaran's 21,834-foot North Peak and the 22,205-foot South Peak. The first ascent of Huascaran's South Peak was made in 1932 by a German-Austrian party.

Among the less difficult high peaks in the Cordillera Blanca are Nevado Copa (20,351 feet) and Nevado Pisco (about 19,000 feet), but even on these peaks climbers may run into dangerous cornices and crevasses. The more difficult climbs include Nevado Cayesh (18,770 feet), an incredible-looking dagger-shaped pinnacle, and Chacraraju (20,055), a twin-headed peak from whose razor-sharp connecting ridge fall

MAP 17. NORTHERN CORDILLERA BLANCA, PERU

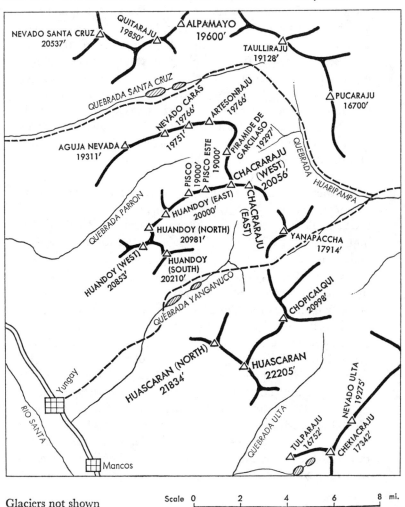

Glaciers not shown

Scale 0   2   4   6   8 mi.

precipitous walls of fluted ice. One of the most famous and most beautiful peaks in the range is 19,600-foot Alpamayo, which, when seen from a certain angle, is an extremely steep, completely white, and faultlessly symmetrical pyramid. The best time of year for climbing in the Cordillera Blanca is June through August, which is the dry season.

Hikers can find interesting trails over the passes of the Cordillera Blanca, or they might prefer to explore the Cordillera Negra, which is just across the valley of the Santa River from the Cordillera Blanca. The Cordillera Negra offers easy climbs of peaks up to 16,000 feet as well as unsurpassed views of the Cordillera Blanca.

Southeast of the Cordillera Blanca there is another range which is comparable to it in grandeur, though not in extent: the Cordillera Huayhuash. This range contains Peru's second highest peak, 21,759-foot Yerupaja, noted for its steep ice walls and treacherous cornices.

The Cordillera Blanca and the Cordillera Huayhuash are the most impressive Peruvian ranges, but there are several others which are only slightly less magnificent. These include the Cordillera Vilcanota (highest peak; 20,945-foot Ausangate), southeast of Cuzco; the Cordillera Vilcabamba (19,951-foot Salcantay), northwest of Cuzco; and the Cordillera de Apolobamba (19,830-foot Chaupi Orco), located astride the Peru-Bolivia border. At least seven other more or less distinct Peruvian ranges contain ice peaks over 18,000 feet. Most of these are southeast of, and within 200 miles of, the Cordillera Huayhuash. For a complete breakdown of the Peruvian ranges see *Las 20 Cordilleras Peruanas,* by Cesar Morales Arnao.

Peru also has its share of giant volcanoes in the Cordillera Occidental, which parallels the Pacific coast in the southern part of the country. The highest, Nevado Coropuna (21,702 feet), was first climbed in 1911 by Hiram Bingham, the Yale professor who discovered Macchu Picchu and later became Governor of Connecticut and then a U. S. Senator. The usual route on Coropuna is up the southeast side from the village of Viraco (about 10,500 feet), which is reached by road from Chuquibamba. About five days should be allowed for the round trip from Viraco. The climb is over volcanic ash to the glacier-covered upper slopes, where deep snow may be encountered. Following Coropuna in height are Nevado Solimana (20,744 feet), Nevado Ampato (20,702-feet), and Nevado Chachani (19,931 feet). The well-preserved cone of El Misti (19,098 feet) dominates the city of Arequipa, and for this reason it is one of the best known of Peruvian volcanoes. It is also one of the easiest climbs in the world for its height. The normal route is usually climbed in two days from Chiguata (about 9850 feet). Both Chachani and El Misti were climbed by the Incas, who left a tomb on the summit of the former, and a temple on the latter. The Spaniards placed a cross on El Misti as early as 1784, and its summit has even been used as a weather observation post. The Cordillera Occidental borders Peru's extremely dry coastal strip and has much less precipitation than the inland ranges, which receive most of their moisture from the Amazon basin. As a result, even 19,000-foot mountains like El Misti are almost snow-free.

▲ ECUADOR ▲

Between 1736 and 1744, at a time when scientific interest in mountains was just dawning, a remarkable Franco-Spanish expedition conducted a very thorough study of the mountains of Ecuador. Their most notable discovery was a mountain higher than any other known to the Western world at that time—Chimborazo—and for the next three-quarters of a century this 20,561-foot mountain was believed to be the highest on earth. In a sense, Chimborazo can still be considered the "highest," because its elevation combined with its location near the earth's equatorial bulge, make its summit the farthest in the world from the center of the earth.

The northern half of Ecuador has without doubt the most impressive collection of volcanoes to be found anywhere. In outline, the Andes here consist of two parallel chains of volcanoes, one on the east and one on the west, between which is an elongated plateau. This is the narrowest part of the Andes, and it is less than 100 miles from the steaming lowlands of the Amazon basin to the equally steaming lowlands on the Pacific side. The most important peaks of the western chain are, from north of south: Cotacachi (16,204 feet), Pichincha (15,696 feet), Illiniza (17,277 feet), and Chimborazo (20,561 feet); the eastern chain claims Cayambe (18,996 feet), Antisana (18,717 feet), Cotopaxi (19,347 feet),

MAP 18.   CHIMBORAZO, ECUADOR

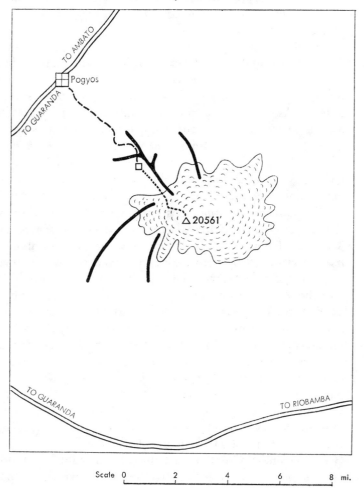

TO AMBATO

Pogyos

TO GUARANDA

△ 20561'

TO GUARANDA

TO RIOBAMBA

Scale 0   2   4   6   8 mi.

Tungurahua (16,457 feet), Altar (17,457 feet), and Sangay (17,159 feet). There are in addition a number of other volcanoes over 14,000 feet.

Chimborazo was first climbed in 1880 by the Englishman Edward Whymper, of Matterhorn fame, with the brothers Carrel as guides. On the same expedition Whymper also made the first ascents of Cayambe, Antisana, and several lesser peaks, in what was from the standpoint of major first ascents one of the most successful mountaineering expeditions on record; Whymper's adventures are described in *Travels Amongst the Great Andes of the Equator,* which, like his earlier *Scrambles Amongst the Alps,* is one of the classics of mountaineering literature.

The snowline in Ecuador is approximately 15,000 feet in the eastern chain, and 16,000 feet in the dryer western range. Thus all of the higher peaks are snow climbs. Chimborazo itself is crowned by a thick icecap which covers whatever might remain of a crater. The usual route to the summit of Chimborazo is up the northwest side from Pogyos, at about 14,000 feet; Pogyos is reachable by dirt road from Ambato. A trail takes one in half a day from Pogyos to the Plaza Roja hut at approximately 15,750 feet; burros can be hired locally for packing to the hut. From there it takes about three or four hours to climb to Murallas Rojas (red walls), where most parties establish a high camp. Just above, at roughly 18,500 feet, one meets the glacier. From Murallas Rojas, it is probably best to traverse left and then head straight toward the true summit, rather than going directly up over the false (west) summit; Chimborazo's broad, plateaulike summit area is notorious for deep snow, which is particularly bad between the false summit and the true summit. The main problems on Chimborazo are the altitude and the tiring work, but crevasses and possible encounters with steep, crusted snow require a knowledge of snow and ice techniques. Chimborazo is a big mountain and not to be taken lightly. In addition to the route described here, several more technically difficult ice routes have been climbed. On Chimborazo, as well as the other high, snow-capped volcanoes, climbers would be well advised to carry willow wands, because cloudiness is frequent and can make route finding a real problem.

Though 19,347-foot Cotopaxi is in second place in height, many people consider it to be the most majestic mountain in Ecuador. It is a big mountain which rises as high above its base as does Chimborazo. However, its fame is based not on its size but on its Fuji-like symmetry. The first successful ascent of Cotopaxi was that of Wilhelm Reid and A. M. Escobar in 1872. To reach the starting point for the normal route up the north side of Cotopaxi, ordinary cars can be driven as far as Limpio-Pungo at about 13,800 feet. From there jeeps can continue upward to 15,700 feet, where one can make camp; or one can camp a few hundred feet higher at the lower edge of the permanent snow. The climb is up a rather heavily crevassed glacier, and requires experience in snow and ice climbing as well as route finding. The route heads toward a black-rock cliff (Yanasacha), then skirts the cliff to the right, then goes up to the crater rim. Although the mountain has been climbed frequently, the highest point on the crater rim is actually a steep pinnacle which has only been scaled a few times.

Ecuador's third and fourth highest summits, 18,996-foot

Cayambe and 18,717-foot Antisana, are also snow climbs. For Cayambe, cars can reach the farm "La Chimba" of the Junta de Beneficencia de Cayambe, from where a camp on the northwest slope at 15,700 feet can be reached by horse or mule-back. At 16,000 feet on the south side of Cayambe one can stand on the highest point on the Equator. A popular climb with Ecuadorian mountaineers is 17,277-foot Illiniza. Cars can reach about 14,000 feet on the north side of the mountain, and there is a hut at 15,600 feet. Though short and easily accessible from Quito, the climb is relatively difficult.

The most active volcano in Ecuador is 17,159-foot Sangay. The two-day ascent from Hacienda Alao, on the west side, is not technically difficult, but there are inevitable risks in climbing any volcano that might erupt any moment. One party reported that a volcanic bomb six inches in diameter crashed through their tent, just missing the occupants, while others have reported seeing blocks as large as automobiles hurled into the sky.

For climbers interested in a fairly easy climb of moderate height, a suitable goal is 16,457-foot Tungurahua, which is a two-day hike up the north slope from Banos. Guides are available locally; since the last 1500 feet are on snow, crampons are useful. Quito's backyard peak, 15,542-foot Rucu Pichincha, is an easy one-day hike from the city by way of Cruz Loma; it is a good conditioner for the giants and provides a fine view of them. The slightly higher twin-peak Guagua Pichincha (15,696 feet) is also an easy hike. The most spectacular mountain in Ecuador is 17,457-foot Altar, whose top is a segment of the rim of a caldera. One side of the rim has been eroded away, and what remains is a steep, semi-circular "altar" capped by sharp ice-sheathed peaks and pinnacles. For technical climbers, Altar is the most interesting mountain in Ecuador.

The dry season in Ecuador is May through September, while March is the height of the rainy season. Guides for Chimborazo and other climbs in Ecuador can be arranged for through Agrupacion Excursionista "Nuevos Horizontes," P. O. Box 2369, Quito.

▲ COLOMBIA ▲

Sierra Nevada de Santa Marta

The highest coastal mountains on earth are Colombia's Sierra Nevada de Santa Marta, only 1100 miles south of Miami. Here, just 30 miles in from the shores of the Caribbean, the great twin peaks of Cristobal Colon and Simon Bolivar reach the monumental height of 5775 meters (18,947 feet). Although the two summits are of almost identical height, Cristobal Colon is generally shown on maps as the highest in Colombia. The S. N. de Santa Marta is an isolated mountain mass which lies to the west of the main crest of the Andes; the main crest is here known as the Sierra de Perija (highest point 12,303 feet) and forms the boundary between Colombia and Venezuela. The S. N. de Santa Marta is so completely set off from the Sierra de Perija that a 1000-foot rise in the level of the oceans would turn the whole Santa Marta massif into an island.

For mountains so little known and rarely visited, the snowy heights of the S. N. de Santa Marta are not difficult to see. They are visible on a clear day from Barranquilla, 75 miles away, as well as from the closer city of Santa Marta; good views are also obtained sometimes from cruise ships in the Caribbean. Getting into the mountains, however, is a different matter. The approach from the north is virtually impossible because the lower slopes on that side are covered by nearly impenetrable jungle. The usual departure point therefore is the town of Valledupar, which is southeast of the massif; the town can be reached by car or by air from Barranquilla. From Valledupar vehicles can be hired to Atanquez, where mules and porters should be available. It is about a four-day trek from Atanquez up the valley of the Donachui River to a possible camp site at 15,000-feet-plus at the base of the cirque on the southeast side of Cristobal Colon and Simon Bolivar.

Pico Cristobal Colon has been climbed both by its east ridge and by way of the 18,200-foot saddle between it and Simon Bolivar. The east ridge route involves both rock and snow climbing of moderate difficulty, but is probably easier than the saddle route, which is primarily a snow climb. The first ascent of Cristobal Colon was made by an American party in 1939, a few weeks after a German party made the first ascent of Simon Bolivar.

Cristobal Colon and Simon Bolivar are near the western edge of the S. N. de Santa Marta. East of them the main

MAP 19. S. N. DE SANTA MARTA, COLOMBIA

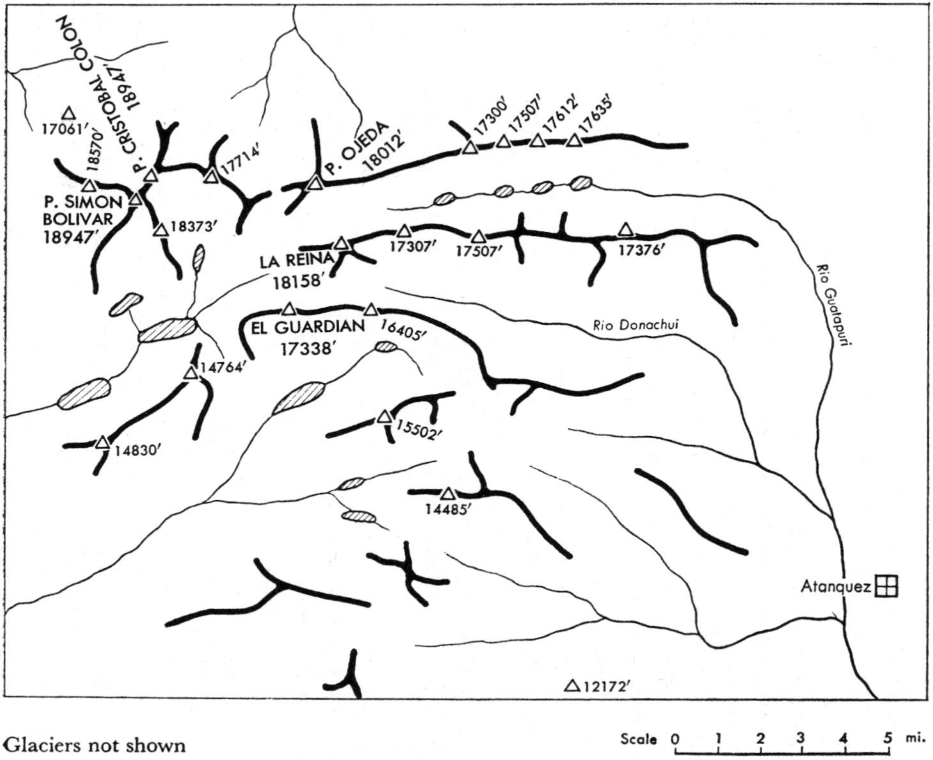

P. CRISTOBAL COLON 18947'

17061'
18570'

P. SIMON BOLIVAR 18947'

18373'

1714'

P. OJEDA 18012'

14764'

14830'

LA REINA 18158'

EL GUARDIAN 17338'

16405'

17307'

17507'

15502'

14485'

17300'
17507'
17612'
17635'

17376'

Rio Guatapuri

Rio Donachui

12172'

Atanquez

Scale 0 1 2 3 4 5 mi.

Glaciers not shown

peaks are strung along three parallel ridges which run east to west. The high point of the northern ridge is Pico Ojeda (18,012 feet); the central ridge, which is noted for its heavy glaciation, reaches 18,158 feet in La Reina; the southern ridge is topped by 17,338-foot El Guardian. The Donachui valley lies between the central and southern ridges. South of the ridge containing El Guardian there are a number of rock towers, some over 15,000 feet; here rock climbers can find interesting and difficult climbing on good granite.

Although the S. N. de Santa Marta must be considered first of all a paradise for climbers, hikers will find the valleys between the peaks delightful; these valleys are noted for their beautiful glacial lakes. The snowline in the range is about 16,500 feet on the southern slope and 16,000 feet or less on the north. The best time for climbing is the winter dry season, December to March, with January considered the ideal month; next best is the summer dry season, June to August.

Sierra Nevada de Cocuy

The S. N. de Santa Marta is not the only range of alpine mountains in Colombia. Just south of the Venezuelan border is the Sierra Nevada de Cocuy, which is the most heavily glaciated range in Colombia. Because its icy summits rise directly above the steaming jungle lowlands of the Orinoco basin, the S. N. de Cocuy is enshrouded in mist most of the time; in this respect it has been compared to the Ruwenzori of Africa and the Snow Mountains of New Guinea. The mist creates a protective shield which causes the snowline to drop a thousand feet lower than in the S. N. de Santa Marta.

The S. N. de Cocuy consists of two parallel ridges which run north and south, with the higher summits on the western ridge; the highest peak is 18,023-foot Alto Ritacuba. The peaks of the S. N. de Cocuy are characterized by steep rock faces on the east and relatively gentle, snow-covered slopes on the west. The biggest problem in climbing these mountains is the almost perpetual bad weather and mist, which make route-finding difficult. The best climbing weather in the S. N. de Cocuy is during the winter "dry season"—if such a term can be used for this area—which is likely to last from December to March. The weather on the eastern side of the range is even worse than on the western.

The approach to the western foot of the S. N. de Cocuy is quite easy. The town of Cocuy, just seven airline miles from Alto Ritacuba, can be reached by bus or car in one long day from Bogota. From Cocuy a cultivated valley only two or three miles west of the crest of the western ridge is now accessible by road. Despite the relative ease of access, Alto Ritacuba was not climbed until 1942. As of 1968, all the major peaks appear to have been climbed except for Campanilla Chico, a rock tower (ca. 15,700 feet) at the southeast end of the range. Rock climbers have found that the rock (gneiss) in the S. N. de Cocuy is bad for climbing.

Other Mountains in Colombia

With the exception of the S. N. de Santa Marta, which stands apart, the Andes of Colombia are divided into three ranges: the Cordillera Oriental, the Cordillera Central, and the Cordillera Occidental. The Cordillera Oriental reaches its greatest height in the S. N. de Cocuy; a little farther north the range splits, with the western branch becoming the Sierra de Perija (mentioned above) and the eastern branch heading into Venequela where it becomes the Sierra Nevada de Merida. The Cordillera Occidental reaches 15,650 feet in Nevado de Cumbal, just north of the Ecuadorian border, but farther north the highest summits are only about 13,000 or 14,000 feet. The Cordillera Central is bounded by the Rio Cauca on the west and the Rio Magdalena on the east. It is in this range that one finds the great snow-capped volcanoes of Colombia. The highest is probably the heavily glaciated, four-peaked Nevado del Huila (height probably under 18,000 feet though many maps show 18,865 feet). Nevado del Ruiz (about 17,450 feet) is easily accessible from Manizales. About 16 miles south of Ruiz is Nevado de Tolima (*ca.* 16,700 feet), which has on its north side a heavily crevassed slope crowned by a steep ice wall; this face of the mountain appears not to have been climbed, as of 1968. Between Ruiz and Tolima is Nevado Santa Isabel (*ca.* 16,570 feet), another snow and ice climb. (Note: there is considerable discrepancy among various sources about the heights of Colombia's volcanoes.)

▲ VENEZUELAN ANDES ▲

Venezuela is not usually thought of as one of the major Andean countries, and, to be sure, its mountains are not as high as those of the countries to the south. However, the Sierra Nevada de Merida, the highest portion of the Venezuelan Andes, is a range of alpine rock and ice peaks which ranks as one of the important mountaineering centers of the Andes. For the "Norteamericano," the mountains of Venezuela are by far the most accessible of the high Andes, and residents of the U. S. East Coast can climb in them in no more time than it takes for a trip to the American Rockies.

The Andes in Venezuela consist of two parallel ridges which run from the Colombian border northeastward toward Caracas. The western ridge reaches 15,590 feet in Piedras Blancas, 20 miles northeast of the town of Merida, and just 30 miles from the shores of Lake Maracaibo. The eastern ridge, the Sierra Nevada de Merida, is just southeast of Merida and contains Venezuela's highest peak, 16,427-foot Pico Bolivar, as well as three other peaks over 16,000 feet—16,210-foot Pico Humboldt, 16,144-foot La Concha, and 16,020-foot Pico Bonpland. Merida, at 5200 feet in the long valley between the two ridges, enjoys a climate of perpetual spring and is Venezuela's main mountain resort.

MAP 20. PICO BOLIVAR, Venezuelan Andes

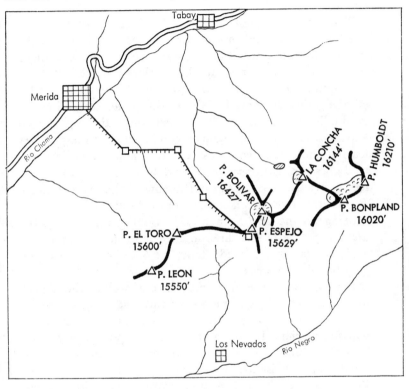

Tabay

Merida

Rio Chama

P. BOLIVAR
16427'

LA CONCHA
16144'

P. HUMBOLDT
16210'

P. BONPLAND
16020'

P. EL TORO
15600'

P. ESPEJO
15629'

△P. LEON
15550'

Los Nevados

Rio Negro

Scale 0   1   2   3   4   5   6 mi.

Merida is reached by good roads and by daily flights from Caracas.

The world's highest cable car (*teleferico*) starts from the edge of Merida, and in one hour climbs 10,400 feet to the terminal on the summit of 15,629-foot Pico Espejo, a minor peak a little over a mile to the southwest of Pico Bolivar. The summit of Pico Espejo is the usual starting point for climbing Pico Bolivar. For those who prefer to acclimatize gradually and savor the scenery en route, the top of Pico Espejo can also be reached by a good trail in two days. After leaving the cultivated fields behind at about 7000 feet, the trail goes through dense rain forest to timberline at 10,000 feet, above which is the *paramo* (the zone of alpine vegetation). A compromise between starting out cold at 15,629 feet and walking all the way from Merida would be to get off the *teleferico* at one of the three intermediate stations and start walking from there. Incidentally, the *teleferico* is in operation only five days a week.

Pico Bolivar is the most impressive as well as the highest mountain in the range; it is a steep three-sided pyramid with sharp, jagged ridges, high rock walls, and a number of hanging glaciers. Its first ascent, that of a Venezuelan party in 1935, came after many unsuccessful attempts. On the usual route (Weiss Route) up the peak there is a trail from Pico Espejo as far as the snout of the Timoncito Glacier; the trail goes down to about 15,000 feet before starting back up. Above this glacier, a large gully leads up Bolivar's south face; during the dry season this gully is largely snow-free. Parties with inexperienced climbers should rope up at the beginning of the gully. One follows the gully in the direction of the east ridge, but before the crest is reached the route veers up a smaller gully which angles left toward the southwest ridge. A gap in this ridge opens onto the northwest face, where a series of easy but exposed ledges leads to the summit. The route is more than just rock scrambling, but strong hikers should have little trouble if they are in a roped party with a guide or experienced leader. Climbers in good condition can make the ascent in one day from Merida by taking the earliest *teleferico* in the morning and returning by the last one in the afternoon. Otherwise, it is a two-day trip, and climbers can spend the night at a hut near the Pico Espejo terminal, but it is (1977) in poor condition.

The second highest peak in Venezuela, Pico Humboldt, can be climbed in two days from Pico Espejo by way of the large glacier on its western slope. Although not among the highest peaks in the range, Pico El Toro (15,600 feet) and Pico Leon (15,550 feet) and the two most prominent summits as seen from Merida; both are easy one-day hikes from the Pico Espejo terminal.

The dry season in the Venezuelan Andes is December through April. During the wet season, June to October, there is heavy snow, and some skiing is done at Pico Espejo; however, there is as yet no tow. The lower limit of the glaciers is about 15,000 feet.

Permission to hike or climb in the Sierra must be obtained from the headquarters of the Parque Nacional Sierra Nevada and from the Comisión Regional de Defensa Civil.

There are three small mountaineering clubs in Merida. The most active seems to be Club Cóndor. There are also clubs centered in Caracas.

▲ ANTARCTICA ▲

Most of Antarctica's vast surface is a plateau of ice averaging over a mile above sea level, which makes it by far the highest of continents. Without the ice, however, Antarctica's average elevation would be greatly reduced, and a good portion of what appears on maps as part of the continent would turn out to be under water; in fact, the continent's highest range, the Ellsworth Mountains, would be on an island.

The highest part of the Ellsworth Mountains is called the Sentinel Range, whose two highest peaks are the Vinson Massif (16,860 feet) and Mt. Tyree (16,290 feet). Both of these peaks and several others were first climbed by an American expedition in December 1966 and January 1967. An airplane landed the expedition on the flat surface of the ice sheet 20 miles west of the mountains, and from there the climbers transported their equipment to the base of the peaks on sleds. The Sentinel Range's western escarpment, which the expedition faced as they approached the mountains, is extremely steep. Mt. Tyree, perhaps the most spectacular peak in the range, rises all the way to its summit in one unbroken sweep from the flat 9000-foot-high surface of the ice sheet. The Vinson Massif itself is a bulkier mountain which turned out to be easier to climb than some of the others, including Tyree. Although this highest peak in Antarctica was not discovered until 1957, the thoroughness of Antarctic exploration since then has clearly ruled out the possibility that elsewhere in the continent's vast empty spaces there may be still higher undiscovered peaks—much less mountains to top the Himalayas, as some people once conjectured.

The continent's highest mountains outside of the Sentinel Range appear to be in the Queen Maud Range, which tops 14,000 feet. But perhaps the best-known Antarctic mountain aside from the Vinson Massif is Mt. Erebus, the continent's only known active volcano, which is just a little over 20 miles from the U. S. station in McMurdo Sound. This 12,450-foot peak was discovered in 1841, and climbed by members of the Shackleton party in 1908.

▲ SOUTHERN WATERS ▲

In the South Atlantic and the southern Indian Ocean there are a number of islands with peaks ranging from 3000 to over 9000 feet in elevation. Though well north of the Antarctic Circle, and in latitudes comparable to northern Europe, these islands have some of the world's worst weather, and climbing on them requires an effort of Himalayan proportions.

South Georgia is one of the most rugged lands on earth.

It is almost entirely mountainous and although at only 54° south latitude it is largely covered by glaciers, many of which reach the sea. The highest peak, 9625-foot Mt. Paget, was not climbed until 1964 (though a party in 1960 reached a lower summit of the mountain). Grytviken, a permanent whaling settlement on the north coast of the island, is served by a shipping line from the Falkland Islands.

Heard Island, at 53° latitude in the Indian Ocean, is occupied almost entirely by a 9005-foot volcano named Big Ben. The island's climate can be described as a nearly perpetual blizzard. One of the problems climbing parties have faced has been that the sea has often been too rough to allow them even to make a landing on the island. Glaciers reach the sea around most of the island's circumference. There were several attempts to climb the mountain before the first successful one in 1965. But even the 1965 party had to wait many days for a spell of decent weather in which to make the climb, and by the time they started down the weather had closed in again, making it difficult to find the route even though they had used route markers on the way up. Technically the climb was not difficult. Despite the forbidding weather, American whalers used Heard Island for a time during the 19th century, and from 1948 to 1955 the Australians maintained a meteorological station there; however, there is no permanent settlement.

The Kerguelen Islands, a French possession northwest of Heard Island, are slightly more hospitable, and the French maintained a permanent scientific group there in recent years. But the weather on the mountains is still bad and the highest peak, 6430-foot Mt. Ross, was unclimbed as of 1967;

this spectacular rock and ice peak is part of the eroded rim of an old volcanic crater.

The Crozet Islands (west of the Kerguelens) are a small, uninhabited group of mountainous islands. The mountain on East Island is 6542 feet and it has probably not been climbed (as of 1967). The Prince Edward Islands, 600 miles west of the Crozet Islands, reach 3890 feet on Marion Island.

If there is any place on earth with worse weather than Heard Island, it is probably Bouvet Island, a Norwegian possession at 54° latitude in the South Atlantic. The island consists of nothing more than a 3068-foot-high volcano and is almost completely covered by ice, right down to sea level. The mountain is probably unclimbed.

The South Orkney Islands and the South Shetland Islands are both mountainous; the former reach 7200 feet on Coronation Island, and the latter reach 7546 feet on Clarence Island. Politically, as well as geographically, the two groups can be considered part of Antarctica; that is, they are south of 60° latitude, which makes them international territory under the terms of a 1959 treaty which set aside Antarctica as an international scientific preserve.

▲ ATLANTIC OCEAN ▲

Canary Islands

Pico del Teide in the Canary Islands is the highest mountain in the Atlantic Ocean, though the early seafarers who thought it was the highest on earth have long since been proven wrong. From any direction, Teide's 12,128-foot leap out of the ocean is an impressive sight, but the slopes are steepest on the northern side where the summit is only 10 miles from the water's edge. The present peak of Teide rises out of the caldera of an older collapsed volcano; a portion of the rim of the caldera can still be seen on the south side, where it forms a long steep ridge called Las Canadas.

Teide is an easy day's climb and one can in fact ride a mule up the summit trail. The trail begins at Lomo Tieso (near Montana Blanca) at 8000 feet on the southeast slope of the peak. The starting point of the trail is reached by road from Santa Cruz de Tenerife. Viewing the sunrise from the summit is a local tradition, and many hikers therefore divide the trip into two days, spending the night at the Alta Vista Hut at 10,700 feet. From the summit on a clear day one can see not only all of the island of Tenerife, which Teide dominates, but also the entire archipelago of the Canaries. Teide can be climbed any time of year, but one should be prepared for snow between October and May.

Cape Verde Islands

The highest mountain in the Cape Verde Islands is the volcano Pico da Cano (9281 feet) on Fogo Island.

Azores

The highest mountain in the Azores is "Pico" (7615 feet), a symmetrical volcanic cone which dominates the island of "Pico." From Madalena a road leads six miles to a little over 4000 feet elevation, from where the gentle slopes can be easily followed to the summit. However, there is no trail, and when it is foggy one must be careful to locate the end of the road on the descent, otherwise he will get into thick shrub. "Pico" is sometimes snow covered in winter.

Fernando Poo

The island of Fernando Poo, off the coast of Cameroon, is topped by the volcano Pico de Santa Isabel (9869 feet). A motor road was recently built to the summit of the peak in connection with the construction of a television tower there. The dry season, November through March, offers the best hope for a view across the Bight of Biafra to Mt. Cameroon, 50 miles away. Fernando Poo's best-known scenery is its lovely crater lakes.

Tristan de Cunha

At 37° south latitude the volcanic island of Tristan de Cunha rises abruptly out of the Atlantic Ocean to a height of 6760 feet. The island has a permanent town, which attracted worldwide attention in the early 1960's when it was evacuated for a year and a half because of renewed volcanic activity. "The Peak," which occupies all but a tiny corner of the island, is an easy hike.

Trinidad Islands

Climbers looking for something unusual might consider an expedition to the Trinidad Islands, some 650 miles off the coast of Brazil. One island, Il Monumento, is described as a rock pillar which thrusts out of the water to a height of 800 feet.

▲ THE FAR NORTH ▲

Greenland

The interior of Greenland is a vast plateau of ice which in places is over 10,000 feet thick. At the outer edges of the icecap, however, there is some magnificent mountain scenery, particularly near the southeast coast, where climbers have found peaks and aiguilles offering face climbs up to 4000 feet in height. The highest peak in Greenland, Gunnbjorn (12,139 feet), was first climbed in 1935 by a British expedition.

Iceland

The mountains of Iceland are characterized by two things —ice and fire. Most of the ice is locked up in a few fairly sizable icecaps of which the Vatnajökull, covering 3400 square miles, is the largest. The mountains which these icecaps crown are volcanoes, and some of them are still active; on several occasions in the past the fires of the volcanoes have melted the glaciers and sent disastrous torrents down onto lowland settlements. The highest summit in Iceland is Hvannadalshnuker (6952 feet), which is on the rim of the crater of Öraefajökull, an ice-capped volcano that connects with the southern edge of the Vatnajökull. From the south, where Fagurholsmyri is the starting point, the climb can be made in one very long day. The glacier is reached at 3500 feet, and the rim of the crater at 6000 feet. Then there is a fairly level three-mile walk across the ice-filled crater floor before the final 1000-foot ascent. There are crevasses en route, so parties must be properly equipped for glacier travel. Mountaineering in Iceland has a long history as evidenced by the fact that the Icelandic doctor and naturalist Sveinn Palsson reached the southern edge of the crater rim of Öraefajökull in 1794.

Jan Mayen

At 71° in the North Atlantic the volcanic cone of Beerenberg juts out of the icy waters to a height of 7472 feet. The volcano occupies most of the island of Jan Mayen and is almost entirely glacier covered. Since the first ascent in 1921,

Beerenberg has been climbed several times by crew members from the Norweigan radio and meteorological station on the island. The climb is reputed to present few technical difficulties, though the weather is usually bad. There is no regular commercial transportation to Jan Mayen, but occasionally a ship brings supplies or replacements for the station crews.

Svalbard

Climatically more hospitable than Jan Mayen, strangely enough, are the main islands of Svalbard, despite the fact that they are 400 miles nearer the Pole. Regular shipping services in summer and fairly frequent flights in the winter serve the 1000 or so permanent residents of Longyearbyen, and there is an influx of summer tourists to this most northerly beneficiary of the Gulf Stream. Numerous climbing expeditions have visited the islands, whose highest summits are Newtontoppen and Perriertoppen (both about 5630 feet) on Vestspitsbergen, the largest island of the archipelago.

Canadian Arctic

There are some very rugged mountains on the islands of the Canadian Arctic, particularly Axel Heiberg and Baffin. Mt. Asgard (6600 feet), on Baffin Island, is one of the world's most unusual and spectacular mountains. It is a great flat-topped rock pillar with nearly vertical walls 3000 feet high on three sides; on the fourth is a sheer drop of 500 feet to a knife-edge ridge which adjoins a neighboring peak.

▲ BRITISH ISLES ▲

In elevation the mountains of Britain are not impressive, but outside of the European Alps and Japan, it is doubtful that any other mountains have played host to more mountaineering activity. Certainly no other mountains have been more minutely described in print.

While rock climbing is the main activity in the British hills, the Scottish mountains in winter present alpine conditions, and in the remoter parts of the Highlands winter climbing can present genuine wilderness experiences. Rock climbing ranges from short but very difficult ascents on sandstone outcrops away from the mountain areas, and similar climbs on sea cliffs, to longer routes in North Wales, the Lake District, and Scotland. All these routes are well documented, and many of the 150-200 climbing clubs have their own guide books, which use standard classifications of routes.

Aside from rock climbing the other main activity in the British mountains is "hill-walking." This is no different from what Americans call hiking, but the particular British combination of lakes, moors, farms, woods, hills, and hospitality gives the sport such a distinctive nature that a different and characteristically British name for it seems justified.

The highest peak in Britain, 4406-foot Ben Nevis, is in Scotland; it is an easy walk from Glen Nevis near Fort William.

But for rock climbers, the 1400-foot northeast face of the peak is one of Britain's most impressive, and it offers many challenging routes, particularly in winter. Some of the finest rock climbing in the British Isles is found on the Scottish Isle of Skye, where the Cuillin Hills reach 3309 feet in Sgur Alasdair. In North Wales there is excellent rock climbing in Snowdonia, where Snowdon reaches 3560 feet, and there are many other hills of the order of 3000 feet. In the Lake District the hills are nearly as high, reaching 3210 feet in Scafell Pike, the highest point in England. The Pennines, running up the center of Northern England, provide excellent mountain walks and plenty of interest for the rock climber.

In Ireland, Carrantuohill (3414 feet) in Macgillicuddy's Reeks, near the southwest tip of Ireland, is the highest point. The hills are excellent walking country.

▲ NORWAY ▲

Norway's fame as one of the most scenic lands on earth does not come solely from its fjords. It is also one of the most mountainous of countries, and although the highest point is only a little over 8000 feet, the mountains have a ruggedness and alpine beauty that is rarely equaled. Nevertheless, despite the ruggedness of most of Norway's mountains, the two highest peaks, Galdhopiggen (8097 feet) and Glittertind (8045) feet), are easy to climb. These two peaks are in the Jotunheimen ("Home of the Giants"), some 150 miles northwest of Oslo, and face each other across the Visdalen valley

MAP 21. GALDHOPIGGEN, Norway

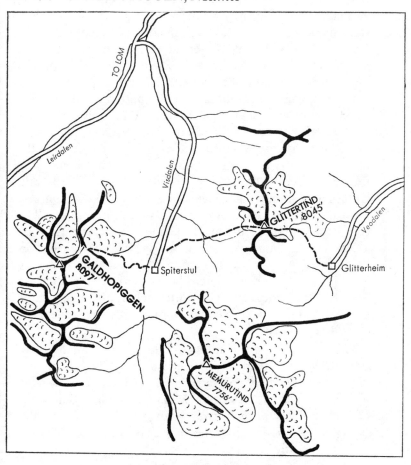

TO LOM

Leirdalen

Visdalen

Veodalen

GLITTERTIND
8045'

GALDHOPIGGEN
8097'

☐ Spiterstul

☐ Glitterheim

MEMURUTIND
7756'

Scale 0   1   2   3   4   5   10   mi.

Galdhopiggen is accepted as the higher peak though a look at some recent Norwegian maps might lead to confusion, since its height is given as 2469 meters, one meter less than Glittertind's 2470. But Glittertind's claim to first place is generally denied because it rests solely on the strength of a 100-foot-deep summit snowbank.

Galdhopiggen's summit is the culmination of a long ridge which rises gently from the east but drops off steeply to the west. The starting point for the normal route is Spiterstul (3600 feet), in the Visdalen valley at the east foot of the mountain. From Spiterstul, which can be reached in a day by train and bus from Oslo, there is a cairned trail to the summit. Guides and special equipment are not needed but climbers must be prepared for snowstorms, even in midsummer. The climb takes about four hours up and two down. The first ascent of Galdhopiggen was made in 1850 by three Norwegians, L. Arnesen, S. Flotten, and S. Sulheim, following what is now the normal route. The usual route up Glittertind is a cairned footpath from Glitterheim, just east of the mountain at 4500 feet, but the climb can also be made quite easily from Spiterstul.

The early history of climbing in Norway is intimately associated with the name of the Englishman Wm. J. Slingsby, whose book *The Northern Playground* helped win him the title of "The Father of Norwegian Mountaineering." Slingsby's years of exploration in Norway were climaxed in 1876 with the ascent of another Jotunheimen peak, 7887-foot Skagastolstind, the third highest in the country. The climb of this giant is still considered no mean feat.

To the west of the Jotunheimen is the Jostedal Glacier,

which covers 300 square miles and is the largest in Europe. The glacier is primarily a large flat icecap at approximately 6500 feet elevation, and is estimated to be 1000 feet thick at the center. The crossing of the glacier is a popular excursion, and regular guided crossings are offered during the summer.

For rock climbers, almost anywhere in Norway has possibilities. Two of the most interesting regions are the Romsdal area near Andalsnes and the Lofoten Islands. Romsdal claims some Matterhorn-like peaks and gigantic rock walls up to 4000 feet high. The Lofoten Islands offer great rock peaks and pinnacles which rise 2000 to 4000 feet right out of the sea. They have been described as an island version of the Chamonix aiguilles.

All the important climbing regions of Norway are described in detail in the guidebook *Mountain Holidays in Norway,* compiled by Per Praag for the Norway Travel Association, Oslo.

▲ SPAIN ▲

Sierra Nevada

Outside of the Caucasus and the Alps, the loftiest mountain in Europe is 11,421-foot Mulhacen in the Sierra Nevada of southern Spain. Mulhacen and all the other high peaks of the Sierra are located southeast of Granada, along a high ridge which for about 10 miles does not drop below 9500 feet. This high crest is only 20 miles from the Mediterranean coast, and is an impressive sight from the sea, especially in winter. The slopes on the south side of the crest are relatively gentle, and all the major peaks offer a walking route from that direction. On the north, however, are the steep headwalls of glacial cirques, and here climbers have found roped routes up most of the peaks.

Mulhacen can be climbed in one day from Trevelez, Spain's highest village, which is just southeast of the peak at 5500 feet. Another popular approach to Mulhacen is from the 11,128-foot summit of Veleta, which is three miles west of Mulhacen; Veleta, the second highest peak in the range, is reached by Western Europe's highest road. The route from Veleta to Mulhacen stays just south of the crestline for the most part, in order to avoid a series of pinnacles called the "Crestones." Army General Don Carlos Ibanez e Ibanez de Ibero constructed an observatory for triangulation on Mulhacen's summit in 1879, and may have been the first to climb the peak. The remains of the structure can still be seen. A little over a mile to the northeast of Mulhacen is 11,043-foot Alcazaba, which is perhaps the most majestic peak in the Sierra Nevada, although it too has a gentle south slope.

There are no glaciers remaining in the Sierra, but some snow lasts through the summer; timberline in the region is approximately 7000 feet. The summer climbing season is from June through September, but with many fine days throughout the year, winter climbing is also quite popular.

MAP 22. SIERRA NEVADA, Spain

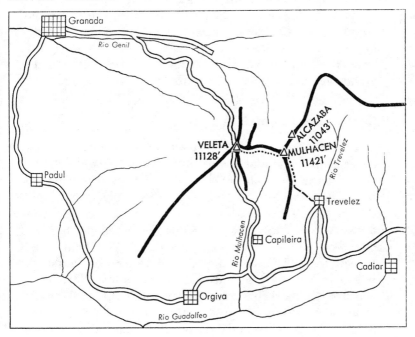

Granada

Rio Genil

Padul

VELETA
11128'

ALCAZABA
11043'

MULHACEN
11421'

Rio Trevelez

Trevelez

Rio Mulhacen

Capileira

Cadiar

Orgiva

Rio Guadalfeo

Scale 0 1 2 3 4 5   10 mi.

Perhaps late spring is the most attractive time to visit the Sierra Nevada, because then one can spend the afternoon swimming in the Mediterranean after a morning of skiing high on the mountains. The Sierra Nevada is well developed for hiking, with an extensive system of trails and huts. Guides are available for either walking tours or rock climbs.

Cantabrian Mountains

The Cantabrian Mountains extend along the northern edge of the central plains of Spain, not far inland from the Bay of Biscay. Near the center of the range and approximately 20 miles from the coast is a group of limestone mountains called the Picos de Europa, which are the steepest rock peaks in Spain. Most of the major summits, including the highest, 8687-foot Torre Cerredo, can be ascended without rope, though even the easiest routes involve steep rock scrambling. But there is no easy way up Naranjo de Bulnes (8385 feet), which is a remarkable columnar monolith with sheer walls on all sides. July and August are the driest and best climbing months in this well-watered region. This is one of the favorite areas of Spanish climbers and it is well served by trails and huts.

Other Spanish Mountains

Central Spain is essentially a vast plain averaging 2000 feet elevation (so it can also be called a plateau), and the major Spanish ranges—the Pyrenees, the Sierra Nevada, and the Cantabrian Mountains—are on its fringes. However, there are also several lesser ranges in the interior where good hiking and climbing can be found. The highest of these are the Sierra de Gredos and the Sierra de Guadarrama. Pico de Almanzor (8504 feet), the highest in the Gredos, is 85 miles west of Madrid, while 7972-foot Pico de Penalara, the highest in the Guadarrama, is just 35 miles north of the city. The granite towers and monoliths of the Pedriza de Manzanare, 25 miles north of Madrid, are popular with rock climbers.

Finally, for anyone interested in combining sightseeing and rock climbing, the historic monastery of Montserrat, near Barcelona, is located amidst some intriguing conglomerate towers and knobs.

▲ PYRENEES ▲

Though the highest summits of the Pyrenees are more than 4000 feet lower than those of the Alps, the average elevation of the high central portion of the former is as high as any comparable section of the latter. Thus the Pyrenean passes are generally quite high, and the range is just as effective a geographic barrier as the Alps. On the north side, the Pyrenees fall steeply to the plains of France, and when seen from that side they appear as a high, fairly even wall. On the Spanish side, however, the slope is less abrupt, and from the plains of Spain the high crest is obscured by foothills.

For climbers the Pyrenees are a very attractive range of mountains with both rock and ice climbing; however, since the glaciers are small the snow and ice climbing cannot be compared to that of the Alps. One of the greatest attractions of the Pyrenees is not the peaks themselves but the large area between timberline and the summits. Timberline averages about 6800 feet while the snowline varies from about 8000 to 9000 feet. For hikers and backpackers who like to wander unroped through alpine high country, the Pyrenees are certainly one of the most appealing regions in Europe.

The highest summit in the Pyrenees is Pico Aneto (11,168 feet). It is the culmination of a granite massif, the Maladeta, which is wholly in Spain and about halfway between the Atlantic and the Mediterranean. The massif is characterized by sharp, sweeping ridges, between which lie the largest glaciers in the range. Pico Aneto was first climbed in 1842 by four local guides and their two clients, a French noble named Albert de Franqueville, and a Russian noble named Platon de Tchihatcheff.

The usual approach to Aneto is from the town of Benasque, seven miles west of the peak at 3700 feet. From the end of a road which leads northeast from the town, a trail leads to La Renclusa Hut at 7000 feet, where most parties spend the night. From the hut the route goes due south across a ridge named Cresta de los Portillones and onto the Aneto Glacier, which is followed to the west ridge; on the ridge there are about 500 yards of rock scrambling and easy rock climbing before the summit is reached. The climb from the hut to the summit takes about five hours. The Aneto Glacier is crevassed, and parties should have rope, crampons, and ice axes; rope

MAP 23.   PICO ANETO, Pyrenees

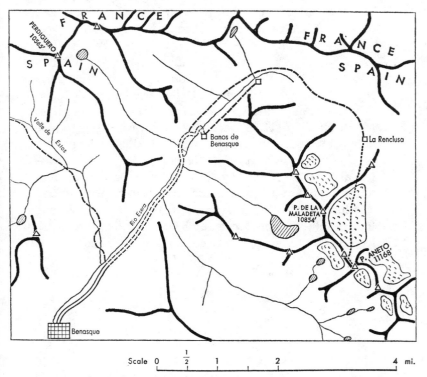

PERDIGUERO
10565'

FRANCE

SPAIN

FRANCE

SPAIN

Valle de Estos

Rio Esera

Banos de
Benasque

La Renclusa

P. DE LA
MALADETA
10854'

P. ANETO
11168'

Benasque

Scale 0   ½   1   2   4 mi.

may also be needed on the summit ridge. Guides are available in Benasque for either this regular route or for a variety of more difficult climbs on the peak.

The second highest peak in the Pyrenees, Pico de Posets (11,073 feet), is a little over 10 miles west of Aneto and can also be climbed in two days from Benasque. The normal route, which starts from the Valle de Estos Hut and climbs by way of the Paul Glacier, requires rope, ice axe, and crampons. Monte Perdido (11,007 feet), 35 miles west of Aneto, is the only other Pyrenean summit over 11,000 feet; the peak can be climbed without rope, though there are also some good technical routes. Other Pyrenean peaks of particular interest to rock climbers are Vignemale (10,800 feet), with its 2500-foot-high north wall; Balaitous (10,322 feet), famed for the traverse of its granite aretes: and Pic du Midi d'Ossau (9466 feet), the steep, pointed core of an eroded volcano.

▲ ALPS ▲

The Alps are the best-known and most written-about mountains on earth, and anyone planning an Alpine vacation should have little trouble finding a great deal of information. In this chapter no attempt will be made to provide thorough or detailed coverage of the Alps; instead, the chapter will merely give a description of the tourist routes up Mont

MAP 24. MONT BLANC, ALPS

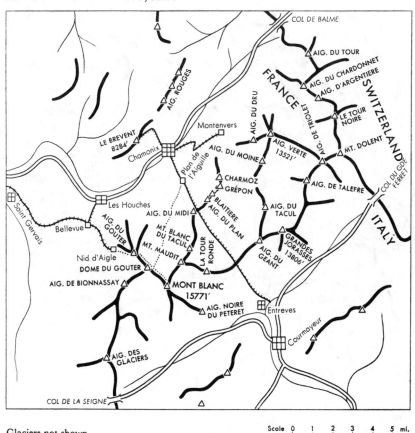

Glaciers not shown

Scale 0 1 2 3 4 5 mi.

MAP 25. MATTERHORN, ALPS

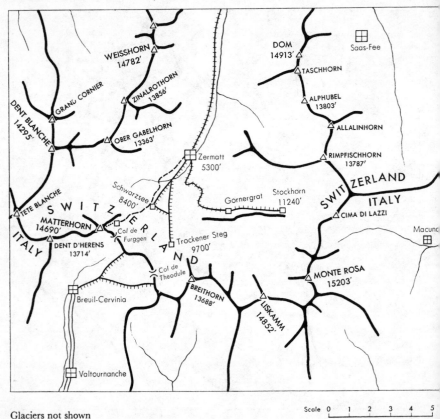

Glaciers not shown

Scale 0 1 2 3 4 5

Blanc and the Matterhorn, the two peaks which are most likely to be the goals of casual climbers on a first trip to the Alps, plus the highest individual summits in each of the Alpine countries.

But first, here for reference is a summarized list of the main sections of the Alps, starting in the west near the Riviera and ending in the east at the outskirts of Vienna: 1. Maritime Alps: shared by France and Italy; highest peak is 10,817-foot Argentera, which is 30 miles inland from Monaco. 2. Cottian Alps: shared by France and Italy; highest peak is 12,602-foot Monte Viso. 3. Dauphine Alps: in France, northwest of the Cottian Alps; highest peaks are the Ecrins (13,461 feet) and the Meije (13,081 feet). 4. Graian Alps: shared by France and Italy; French portion topped by 12,667-foot Grande Casse in the Massif de la Vanoise; highest peak in the Italian portion is 13,323-foot Gran Paradiso. 5. Mont Blanc range: shared by France and Italy, but the summit of Mont Blanc (15,771 feet), the highest point in the Alps, is in France. 6. Pennine Alps: east of Mont Blanc; shared by Switzerland and Italy; contains seven of the nine Alpine peaks over 14,000 feet: Monte Rosa (15,203 feet), Dom (14,913 feet), Lyskamm (14,852 feet), Weisshorn (14,782 feet), Matterhorn (14,690 feet), Dent Blanche (14,295 feet), and Grand Combin (14,154 feet). 7. Bernese Alps: north of the Pennines; topped by the Finsteraarhorn (14,022 feet), but better known are the Jungfrau (13,642 feet) and the Eiger (13,039 feet), with its mile-high north wall, the greatest in the Alps. 8. The Lepontine Alps: east of the Pennine and Bernese Alps; mostly Switzerland, but partly in Italy; highest peak is the Rheinwaldhorn (11,162 feet). 9. Bernina Alps: southeastern Switzerland and northern Italy; highest peak is Piz Bernina (13,284 feet). 10. Ortles group: in Italy, just east of the eastern tip of Switzerland; topped by the Ortles Peak (12,792 feet). 11. The Otztal Alps: along the Austria-Italy border, just east of Switzerland and just north of the Ortles group; highest peak is the Wildspitze (12,382 feet), in Austria. 12. The Dolomites: entirely in Italy; not high for the Alps, but famed for rock climbing on limestone peaks of fantastic form and steepness; highest peak is Marmolata (10,965 feet). 13. Bavarian Alps: shared by Bavaria and Austria; highest peak is the Zugspitze (9721 feet), the highest in Germany. 14. Hohe Tauern: in Austria; divides the provinces of Salzburg and Tirol; topped by Austria's highest peak, 12,457-foot Grossglockner. (From the eastern end of the Hohe Tauern, lower "pre-alpine" mountains and hills extend all the way to the outskirts of Vienna.) 15. Julian Alps: northwestern tip of Yugoslavia, overlapping into Italy; highest peak is Triglav (9393 feet), in Yugoslavia.

The permanent snowline in the Alps varies between 8000 and 9500 feet elevation, depending on latitude and north-south exposure; however, some glaciers extend all the way to 4000 feet and below. Timberline varies from 5500 to 7000 feet. The highest permanently inhabited villages in the Alps are just under 7000 feet.

Mont Blanc

The Mont Blanc range (or massif) consists of Mont Blanc itself and many satellite peaks which are superb mountains in their own right. The range offers some of the best rock and ice climbing in the Alps, and as far as that goes, in the world. The excellence of the firm granite of the Chamonix aiguilles sets a standard by which the rock of mountains everywhere is often compared. The letterhead of the Syndicat des Guides de Chamonix-Mont Blanc (founded in 1821) proclaims Chamonix to be "The greatest center of Alpinism in the entire world," and this is probably accurate. On a good weekend as many as 4000 Alpinists clambor over the crags and glaciers of the Mont Blanc range.

The usual route up Mont Blanc starts at Nid d'Aigle (8116 feet), beside the Bionnassay Glacier on the northwest side of the mountain. Nid d'Aigle is reached by a combination of cable car and train from Les Houches, which is five miles southwest of Chamonix. The usual guided tourist climb is done in two days from Chamonix; on the first day one travels to Nid d'Aigle then hikes in about four-and-a-half hours to the Aiguille du Gouter hut (12,523 feet), where the night is spent. On the second day one climbs to the summit in about five hours, and returns to Chamonix. The descent route is the same down to the Vallot Hut (14,312 feet), but then angles eastward by way of the Col du Dome and the Grands Mulets Hut to the Plan de l'Aiguille (7550 feet) from where a cable car goes directly to Chamonix. This tourist route involves no technical difficulties, though rope, ice axe, and crampons are needed; anyone capable of climbing at nearly 16,000 feet can make the climb with a guide. However, there are considerable dangers for inexperienced climbers without a guide. Bad weather can close in suddenly and on the completely snow-covered upper slopes can cause a severe "white-out";

in such conditions it is easy to lose the route, and even if one does not end up at the bottom of a crevasse, a night out on Mont Blanc can lead to disaster. Guides are readily available, though reservations should be made at least 18 hours in advance; in the height of the season it might be wise to reserve one in advance by writing to the Syndicat des Guides. Crampons and ice axes can be rented in Chamonix, and the guides furnish the rope.

The first ascent of Mont Blanc, by Jacques Balmat and Dr. Paccard in 1786, was one of the landmarks in the history of mountaineering. It was comparable in significance to the conquests of the Matterhorn and Mt. Everest, because it was the first climb of a major mountain in the Alps, and thus was the opening chapter in the whole rich history of Alpinism.

The Matterhorn

If any mountain view is going to take your breath away, the first sight of the Matterhorn rising above the village of Zermatt is it. To the ordinary tourist the Matterhorn looks utterly impossible to climb, but the truth is that it is much easier than it looks. In fact, among experts and especially would-be experts the normal route up the Hornli ridge (the northeast ridge, which faces Zermatt) has the reputation of being "an easy day for a lady." To be sure, even a rich, overweight matron who had never seen a mountain before could hire enough guides to haul her to the top, but if capsulized oxygen is ever developed, it may be possible some day to say the same thing about Mt. Everest. In sum, the normal route up the Matterhorn is easy if you are an experienced technical climber; but if you are a novice, it would be a difficult and very dangerous venture if you tried it unguided—and it is a spectacular and strenuous climb even with a guide. Strong hikers need not hesitate about tackling it, provided they have a professional guide or an equally competent leader, but they must be prepared for 4000 feet of continuous scrambling and moderate rock climbing, some of it very exposed. Arrangements for guides can be made easily in Zermatt.

The normal route up the Matterhorn is usually climbed in two days from Zermatt (5300 feet). On the first day one goes to the Hornli Hut at 10,758 feet, either walking all the way or taking the cable car to Schwarzsee at 8400 feet, and starting from there. Parties leave the Hornli Hut at about 3:00 A.M. the next morning in order to reach the summit by 8:00 A.M. The reason for the early start is to allow time to get down before the midday heat melts the ice that cements rocks to the mountain; the Matterhorn is notorious for loose rock. Guided parties rope up right at the hut and stay roped the whole way. The climb involves little more than scrambling until within a few hundred feet of the summit where there is a stretch of nearly vertical rock with about 4000 feet of exposure; this stretch would halt any but experienced rock climbers were it not for the fact that there is a fixed rope; guided climbers get added security, of course, from the guide's rope. From the top of the steep pitch, an easy but exposed ridge leads to the top. Though one can walk, there is nothing to grasp onto, and to either right or left one could fall nearly a mile. The summit is a narrow ridge shared by Italy and Switzerland.

The first ascent of the Matterhorn, by Edward Whymper

and six other climbers in 1865, brought to a close the "Golden Age of Mountaineering," a decade in which most of the great Alpine peaks were first conquered. The story of the climb, in which four of the seven climbers fell to their deaths on the descent, is probably the best-known tale in the history of mountaineering. Since 1865, the Matterhorn has claimed about 150 lives, but very few accidents have occurred to parties professionally guided; meanwhile, over 60,000 people have safely and successfully enjoyed the ascent of this most spectacular of Alpine mountains.

Monte Rosa

The second highest mountain in the Alps is Monte Rosa (15,203 feet), on the Swiss-Italian border. Its summit is the highest point in both countries. Monte Rosa is 10 miles east of the Matterhorn, and like its more famous neighbor it is accessible in two days from Zermatt; this northern approach involves a relatively easy snow climb similar to that of Mont Blanc.

Zugspitze

The highest point in Germany, the 9721-foot summit of the Zugspitze in the Bavarian Alps, is reached by a cable car. But the Zugspitze remains an impressively rugged mountain which rises over 4000 feet about timberline and carries a couple of small glaciers. The usual hiking route is through the Reintal valley from Garmisch-Partenkirchen. The Bavarian Alps are some of the most frequently climbed and hiked mountains on earth. All the standard routes are well marked with signs and painted markers.

Grossglockner

Austria's highest peak 12,457-foot Grossglockner has some of the biggest glaciers in the Alps. From the town of Heiligenblut, "the Chamonix of Austria," the two-day climb of Grossglockner with a guide is not difficult.

Triglav

Triglav (9393 feet), the highest summit in the Julian Alps and in all Yugoslavia, is usually climbed in two days from Aljazev Dom which is reached by road from Dovie. There is some scrambling and exposure but the climb is suitable for strong hikers; the route is well marked and has fixed cables. Both Triglav and its slightly lower neighbor, 8983-foot Skrlatica, have rock walls with difficult technical routes.

▲ CORSICA & SARDINIA ▲

Corsica is one of the most mountainous islands in the world, and it is an excellent place for a climbing or hiking holiday a little bit off the beaten path. There are fine rock peaks, lovely

MAP 26. MONTE CINTO, CORSICA

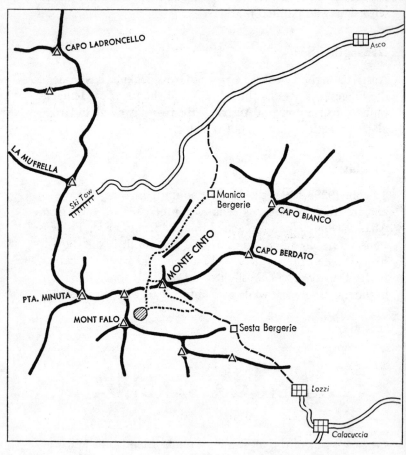

Scale 0   1   2   3   4   5 mi.

forests, steep gorges, and on the west and southeast coasts steep-sided fjordlike bays. For more than half the year the high peaks are covered with snow, and then their white crests are a delightful alpine contrast to the sunny Mediterranean.

The highest peak is Monte Cinto (8891 feet), which is 15 miles inland from the northwest coast. The easiest route to its summit is up the south side from the village of Lozzi (3400 feet), which can be reached via the village of Calacuccia. The climb takes five or six hours and there are no technical difficulties on the normal route, though there is a little rock scrambling near the summit. Guides are available locally. Cinto can also be climbed in a slightly longer day from the north (where Asco is the climbing center). There are some rock routes on Cinto but the really fine rock climbing, of which Corsica has a great deal, is found on the lower neighboring peaks. The Cinto group is the most alpine on the island, and there is a thorough guidebook to it in French— *Le Massif du Cinto,* by Michel Fabrikant. The rainiest months in Corsica are April-May and October-November. June is an excellent time for climbing, since it is between the spring rains and the midsummer heat.

The mountains of Corsica's neighboring island, Sardinia, are not so spectacular. The highest summit, 6017-foot Punta la Marmora in the Gennargentu massif, can be climbed easily on foot or horseback. Monte Limbara (4468 feet), near the northern tip of the island, has granite pinnacles of interest to rock climbers.

▲ APENNINES & THE ITALIAN ▲ VOLCANOES

Apennines

Few climbers outside of central Italy have paid much attention to the Apennines, which, after all, exist in the shadow of their great northern neighbors the Alps. Nevertheless, the range has much to interest climbers, and in the Gran Sasso d'Italia, a massif located only 65 miles northeast of Rome, there are limestone peaks of truly Alpine grandeur. The Gran Sasso reaches 9560 feet in Corno Grande, the highest peak in the entire range.

Corno Grande can be climbed in a short day from the west side. From the town of l'Aquila there is a road to Fonte Cerreto, from where a cable car reaches the ski area of Campo Imperatore at just under 7000 feet. A trail begins here and leads in about four hours to the saddle between Corno Grande and its sister peak, 8650-foot Corno Piccolo. The final portion of the climb is a steep scramble; painted blazes mark the route above the end of the trail. The peak can also be approached from the east by a trail which begins at Pietracamela (3296 feet). Rock climbers can find excellent climbing on both Corno Grande and Corno Piccolo; there are, in fact, no non-roped routes up the latter.

MAP 27. **CORNO GRANDE,** Apennines

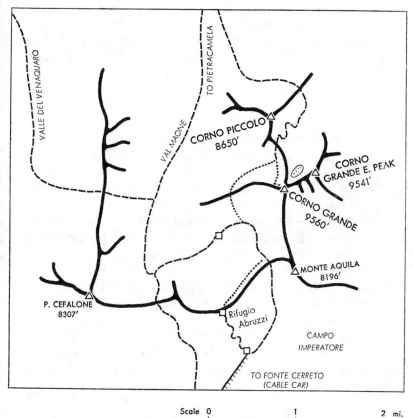

VALLE DEL VENAQUARO

TO PIETRACAMELA

VAL MAONE

CORNO PICCOLO
8650'

CORNO
GRANDE E. PEAK
9541'

CORNO GRANDE
9560'

MONTE AQUILA
8196'

P. CEFALONE
8307'

Rifugio
Abruzzi

CAMPO
IMPERATORE

TO FONTE CERRETO
(CABLE CAR)

Scale 0   1   2 mi.

The high Apennines receive a great deal of snow in winter, and skiing is possible at Campo Imperatore until May. There is even a small glacier on Corno Grande. Good rock climbing can also be found elsewhere in the Apennines, particularly among the sharp rock pinnacles of the Apuan Alps, just north of Pisa.

Mt. Etna

The bulkiest mountain in Europe is Mt. Etna, the 10,741-foot volcano which dominates the island of Sicily. Etna has been active throughout recorded history and has erupted several times in this century. Mt. Etna was undoubtedly one of the first big mountains ever climbed. The Greek philosopher Empedocles (490-430 B.C.) claimed to have climbed it and he was by no means the first. Another early climber was the Roman Emperor Hadrian (A.D. 76-138), who reportedly made the ascent in order to view the sunrise. Today an auto road reaches the Sapienza Refuge at 6288 feet on the south slope, from where a cable car leads to an observatory at 9655 feet. From the observatory the summit is an easy walk of about an hour and a half. If the cable car is not running, the trail from the Sapienza Refuge to the top takes about seven hours round trip. There is also a trail to the summit from the northeast.

Mt. Vesuvius

The most famous volcanic eruption in history was that of Mt. Vesuvius in A.D. 79, which destroyed Pompeii. There have been periodic eruptions ever since, the most recent major one occurring in 1944. A chair lift now takes visitors to just below the 3891-foot summit, which is reached by a short path.

Stromboli

The island of Stromboli consists of little more than the volcano of the same name. In frequent eruption since ancient times, Stromboli is still one of the most active of volcanoes; it regularly gives a reddish glow to the night sky and has been called "The Lighthouse of the Mediterranean." Nevertheless, except during its occasional serious eruptions, the hike to the 3038-foot summit from the village at the base (reached by a weekly steamer) is considered safe.

▲ GREECE ▲

Mt. Olympus

"Olympus" is a name that is familiar to everyone in the Western world, but the Greek mountain which bears it is very little known. To be sure, Greece is known to be a hilly land, but most climbers are surprised to find alpine mountains here and to learn that Mt. Olympus, though only 9570 feet high, has impressive rock walls and snow lasting most of the year.

The ancient Greeks regarded Mt. Olympus—the home of the "gods"—as part mountain and part myth. In one passage in Homer's *Iliad* Zeus talked to the other gods from the topmost peak of "many-ridged Olympus," an apt description. Other writers, however, wrote of the Olympian heights as a cloud-wrapped region far above the surface of the earth. One thing clear is that man had indeed climbed high on the mountain long before the beginning of the Christian era. Convincing evidence for this is the recent discovery of pagan altar fragments and Hellenistic coins on the summit of Agios Antonios (9236 feet), a subsidiary peak of Mt. Olympus located a little over a mile to the south of 9570-foot Mytikas, the highest point. Although the only pre-Christian remains yet found are on Agios Antonios, the remains of Christian chapels from Byzantine times have been found on two other subpeaks, 9550-foot Skolio and 9140-foot Profitis Ilias.

These lesser summits of Olympus must have been visited frequently, but there is no evidence of any ascent of Mytikas before the 20th century. A likely reason for Mytikas' long inviolability is that it is a formidable-looking rock peak which very probably frightened off any potential conqueror until the era of sporting mountaineering. The first modern attempt to reach the highest summit of Mt. Olympus came in 1856 and was followed by several others before two Swiss, Fred Boissonnas and Daniel Baud-Bovy, with the Greek guide Christos Kakalos, finally ascended Mytikas in 1913.

The starting point for the usual route up Mt. Olympus is the town of Litochoron at 1000 feet elevation on the eastern side of the mountain. The town has hotels, restaurants, and

MAP 28. MT. OLYMPUS, Greece

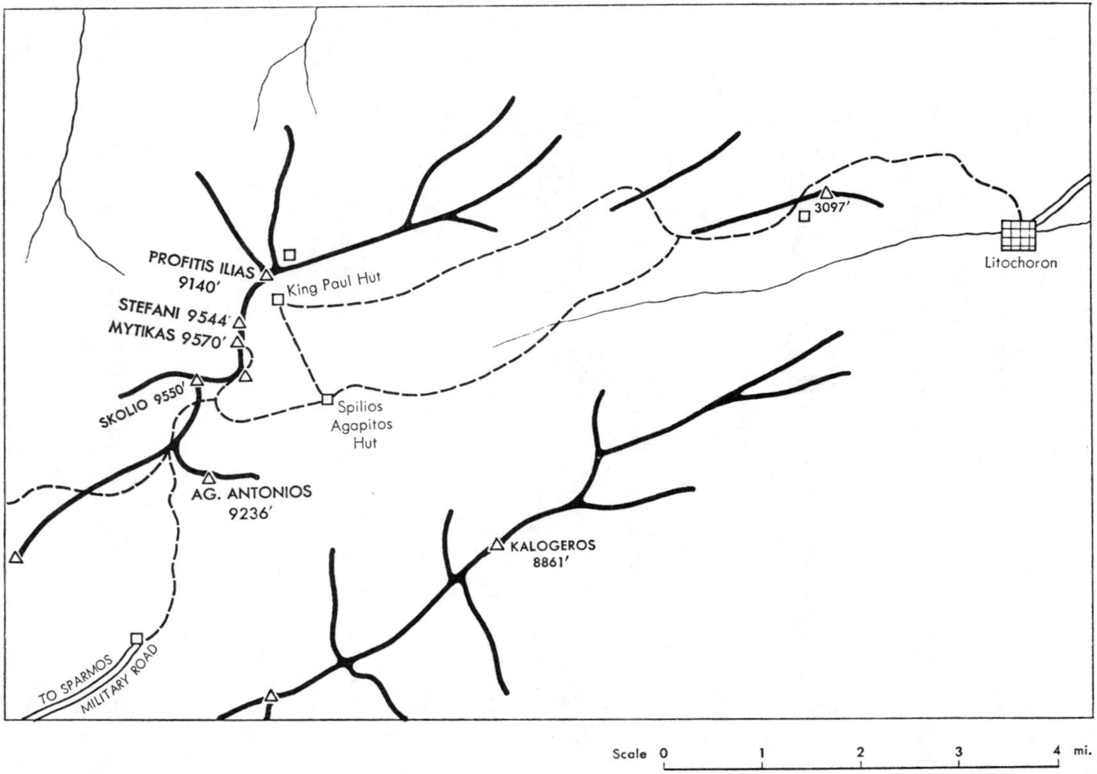

Litochoron

3097'

King Paul Hut

Spilios
Agapitos Hut

PROFITIS ILIAS
9140'

STEFANI 9544'

MYTIKAS 9570'

SKOLIO 9550'

AG. ANTONIOS
9236'

KALOGEROS
8861'

TO SPARMOS

MILITARY ROAD

Scale 0   1   2   3   4 mi.

other facilities, and on the main square one finds the Litochoron branch of the Hellenic Alpine Club. Here arrangements can be made for a guide and pack animals, and for using the Club's huts on the mountain; such arrangements can also be made in advance by mail through the Athens office of the Club: Karageorgi Servias Street, No. 7. From Litochoron there is a trail approximately 12 miles in length to the summit of Olympus. The usual procedure is to hike the first day to Spilios Agapitos Hut at 6900 feet, about 600 feet below timberline. This is a walk of some seven-and-a-half hours over a good trail. From the hut to the summit takes about three-and-a-half hours; although the route is marked with blazes, the terrain is sufficiently rough to warrant novice hikers' hiring a guide. Until late May snow covers some of the upper parts of the trail, making certain exposed spots tricky to cross.

The top of Mt. Olympus should delight the modern alpinist just as it did the ancient gods. It consists of an elongated block of rock with a squarish peak, Stefani (or Thronos Dios), on the north end, and a sharp peak, Mytikas (or Pantheon), on the south. The west face of this block drops sheerly for 1000 feet, and the eastern face is roughly half that. Rock climbers have found many challenging climbs here.

Other Greek Mountains

Four-fifths of Greece is mountainous and there are a number of other peaks that exceed 8000 feet. Mt. Smolikas (8652 feet), which crowns the rugged Pindus Mountains near the Albanian border, is the second highest peak. The eighth highest, 8061-foot Mt. Parnassus, is probably Greece's second most famous mountain because of its role in mythology; the mountain can be climbed by an easy trail in one day from the town of Arachova on the southern slope. The broad, gentle mountains on the island of Crete also reach over 8000 feet in 8058-foot Idhi Oros (Mt. Ida) and 8045-foot Lefka Ori. A trail leads in about five hours from the plateau of Midas to the summit of Mt. Ida.

▲ SOUTHEASTERN EUROPE ▲

The Transylvanian Alps extend east and west across the center of Romania, and at their eastern end meet the southern tip of the Carpathian Mountains. Like the Carpathians, the Transylvanian Alps are primarily a range of forested hills, broken here and there by massifs which rise above timberline, which is about 6000 feet. The highest and most impressive mountains are in the Fagaras massif, the highest peak of which is 8343-foot Moldoveanu, to the northwest of Bucharest. Next to the Tatras, this is the most highly developed mountaineering center in Eastern Europe, and good huts and guides serve a growing number of Romanian climbers who enjoy this region of steep cirques, sharp aretes, and innumerable sparkling glacial lakes. Several other mountains in the Transylvanian Alps also reach 8000 feet, and their rugged beauty rivals that of the Fagaras group.

The highest mountain in Europe between the Alps and the Caucasus is Musala (9596 feet) in the Rhodope Mountains of southern Bulgaria. Musala and several other peaks of nearly equal height rise about 3000 feet above timberline, and some of their substantial winter snowfall lasts throughout the year. The steep cirques and aiguilles of the high Rhodopes provide good climbing amidst spectacular scenery.

Though they have given their name to the entire Balkan peninsula, the Balkan Mountains, which run from east to west across northern Bulgaria, are less impressive than the Rhodopes and other ranges in the region. The range is characterized by rounded summits and alpine meadows on the upper slopes. The highest peak in the Balkan Mountains is Botev (7795 feet), 80 miles east of Sofia. Sofia, it should be mentioned, is ideally situated from the mountaineer's point of view, since it is sandwiched between the Rhodopes on the south and the Balkans on the north.

From the Julian Alps in the north to Macedonia in the south, Yugoslavia is a country of mountains. The highest peak in the country is 9393-foot Triglav in the Julian Alps (see chapter on the Alps). However, the Alps just barely extend across the border into Yugoslavia, and the most important mountains in the country are the Dinaric Alps— which, despite their name, are not considered a part of the "Alpine Alps." The Dinarics are a range of rugged limestone mountains which parallels the Adriatic coast from the vicinity of Trieste all the way to the Albanian border. The forests of these mountains have been ruthlessly exploited through the ages and the coastal mountains are now largely barren, but farther inland there are still enough forests to make Yugoslavia the richest Mediterranean country in terms of timber. The highest and most impressive portion of the Dinarics is in Montenegro, where the major summits rise well above timberline, which is slightly over 6000 feet in the region. The highest peak in Montenegro is 8274-foot Bobotov Kuk (or Cirova Pecina) in the rugged Durmitor group; the peak is a popular one-day climb from the village of Zabljak (4800 feet). In the region where Yugoslavian Macedonia and Albania meet are several small ranges with big mountains. The highest peak, 9068-foot Korab in the Korab Mountains, is on the boundary between eastern Albania and Yugoslavia; it is the second highest point in Yugoslavia and the highest in Albania. The Sar Planina range, in Yugoslavia, reaches 9013 feet in Titov Vrh.

Albania, like Yugoslavia, is a land of rugged mountains. The Albanian Alps in the northern part of the country are structurally an extension of the Dinarics, and their steep peaks and wilderness beauty offer much to both climbers and hikers. The highest peak here is Maje' Jezerce (8838 feet).

▲ CARPATHIANS ▲

The total length of the Carpathian Mountains is about the same as that of the Alps. In the west they begin in central

Czechoslovakia, then follow the Polish-Czechoslovakian border, cross the western tip of the Ukraine, slice down through the middle of Romania, and finally terminate to the northeast of Bucharest. For the most part the Carpathians are wooded hills which are better known for their abundant wildlife than for their alpine scenery. There is, however, one group of spectacular rock mountains of truly alpine proportions, the High Tatras, located on the Polish-Czechoslovakian border 50 miles due south of Krakow. The pinnacles, aretes, and rock walls of these majestic mountains rise as much as 4000 feet above timberline, which averages about 5000 feet (though dwarf pines reach 6500 feet). The range is superb country for hiking, scrambling, or rock climbing. There are many walls offering 1000 or more feet of roped climbing, and the great north face of 8281-foot Maly Kezmarsky is nearly 3000 feet high.

The High Tatras are not extensive in area, stretching only some 30 miles east to west, but their rugged, granite grandeur attracts over a million visitors a year. There are national parks on both sides of the border, and a tourist convention between the two countries allows climbers to cross the border freely to reach their summit goal. Most of the major peaks have "tourist routes" which are not quite rock climbing, yet too steep for walking. Blazes are painted on these routes, and chains and ladders help novices over the tougher spots. The rules of the national parks are that no travel is permitted off of the established trails and marked routes, except by guided or otherwise fully qualified parties. In the Tatras one finds guides of Alpine standard ready to lead him up either the easier routes or the rock walls. There is an extensive system of huts, many of which are located above timberline; camping is permitted only in established campgrounds.

The highest peak in the Tatras, 8737-foot Gerlach, is on a spur on the Czech side of the border. One common route is from the Wielicka Valley, and culminates in a steep ridge scramble. In typical Tatra fashion, the route is well marked and has fixed cables. There is some exposure and caution is required, but the climb is not technically difficult. As with all the major peaks, challenging roped routes can be found on Gerlach. Lomnica (8642 feet), the second highest Tatra peak, can be conquered sitting down: a chair lift goes right up to the summit ridge. Skiing in the Tatras is highly developed, and so is the "apres ski" life.

Although the Tatras have lost their glaciers, they receive a heavy snowfall which lasts through the summer in high, sheltered gullies. Midsummer is often rainy, and the best climbing weather is usually in June and September.

▲ CAUCASUS ▲

As school children learn in geography class, though they may soon forget it, the highest mountain in Europe is not in the Alps, but in the Caucasus. Not so well known is the fact that the Caucasus are a range of mountains as alpine as the Alps. The central Caucasus extend for 120 miles from Elbrus (18,481

MAP 29.   ELBRUS, Caucasus

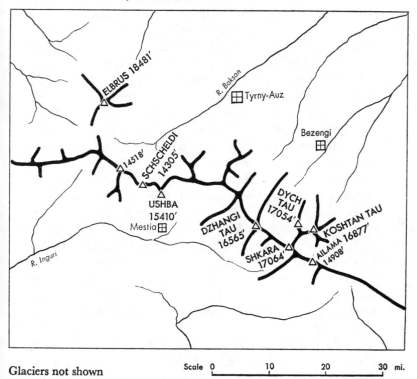

ELBRUS 18481'

R. Boksan

Tyrny-Auz

Bezengi

14518'

SCHSCHELDI
14305'

USHBA
15410'

Mestia

DYCH
TAU
17054'

KOSHTAN TAU
16877'

DZHANGI
TAU
16565'

SHKARA
17064'

AILAMA
14908'

R. Inguri

Glaciers not shown

Scale 0   10   20   30 mi.

feet) on the west to Kazbek (16,558 feet) on the east. These two sentinels are both volcanic cones, but between them runs a chain of steep rock peaks sheathed in ice. The total area of ice in the Caucasus is about half that of the Alps, but the smaller total is due largely to the fact that the Caucasus are narrower, having only one main crest. Though some glaciers in the Caucasus reach as low as 6000 feet elevation, the snowline in the central Caucasus averages about 9500 feet on the north slope and 10,500 feet on the south. This is higher than the snowline in the Alps, but the mountains are also higher and thus rise just about as far above the snowline.

The highest mountain in the Caucasus—Elbrus—is entirely in Europe, being 12 miles north of the watershed which divides Europe from Asia. The gentle slopes of this massive cone culminate in twin peaks, of which the western is 125 feet higher than the eastern. The lower summit was first climbed in 1868 by the English party of Douglas Freshfield, A. W. Moore, and Comyns Tucker, with the guide Francois Devouassoud from Chamonix, and two "native porters." Freshfield did not bother to mention the names of the natives in his book *Travels in the Central Caucasus and Bashan,* but they were the unsung heroes of the conquest. On the summit climb the porters had orginally decided to remain behind at the camp, but later changed their minds and charged after the Alpine veterans. It was bitter cold that morning and after a while the four Western Europeans were on the verge of turning back. At the critical moment the two natives sauntered up, "looking fairly comfortable in their sheepskin cloaks," and their well-timed arrival gave the party just the extra boost it needed. Freshfield's expedition was a landmark in mountaineering history, as it can be said to have opened the era of modern mountaineering beyond the Alps. The higher, western summit of Elbrus was not climbed until 1874, with another English party getting the credit.

Today Elbrus is a popular climb with the Russians, and sometimes hundreds of climbers make the ascent en masse. Climbing is a highly organized activity in the Soviet Union, and most climbing is done during summer camps sponsored by climbing clubs. To reach Elbrus one can travel by train to the town of Naltchik, from where a road leads up the Baksan Valley to the mountain. The upper reaches of the valley are a well-developed mountain-resort area with many camps, lodges, and huts. Vehicles can reach to a short distance below the large hut named the "Refuge of Eleven" on the south slope of Elbrus at over 13,000 feet. From here the climb can be made without technical difficulty provided one stays on the route; off the route there are crevasses. The climb is over snow all the way except for a short stretch near the summit. The main difficulties are the weather and the altitude. Elbrus is, as already noted, north of and detached from the main crest of the range; thus, while one is climbing up the south slope, from below the Refuge of Eleven all the way to the summit, he can see the whole central portion of the Caucasus spread out like a towering mural to the south. The view extends all the way to Kazbek, but some of the most startling mountains are within 20 miles of Elbrus. These include the precipitous two-headed Ushba (15,410 feet), which is generally considered the steepest and most majestic peak in the range, and the sharp rock needles of Schscheldi (14,305 feet).

After Elbrus, the highest peaks in the Caucasus are Shkara (17,064 feet), Dych Tau (17,054 feet), Koshtan Tau (16,877 feet), and Dzhangi Tau (16,565 feet), all of which are within 30 miles east of Ushba. Kazbek, the sixth highest in the range, is situated just west of the Georgia Military Road through the Dariel Pass, the most important pass across the Caucasus. From the town of Kazbek on this road the climb can be made in two or three days, spending one or two nights at a hut at about 12,000 feet. There are no particular technical difficulties, though rope, ice axe, and crampons are needed because the glaciers are crevassed. The first ascent of Kazbek was also made by the Freshfield party.

Although the well-known giants of the Caucasus are all in the central section bounded by Elbrus and Kazbek, the range extends for 600 miles in all, and there is interesting climbing, hiking, and exploring to be found from one end to the other. West of Elbrus, the Caucasus gradually diminish in height, but for 150 miles there continue to be steep rock peaks, the highest of which carry glaciers. This is a beautiful alpine region with extensive virgin forests on the lower slopes. East of Kazbek, the high points are isolated snow-capped mountains. Bazar Dyuzi (14,698 feet), 200 miles from Kazbek and only 60 miles from the Caspian, is the most easterly peak over 14,000 feet. In the moister western Caucasus, which is slightly farther north, the snowline falls to less than 9000 feet; in the dry, barren east it rises to over 12,000 feet.

The Caucasus have long been known to the Western world. Greek sailors spotted them from the Black Sea and thought them to be the highest mountains on earth; Elbrus itself is easily visible from the Black Sea, 70 miles away, on a clear day. According to a Caucasian legend reported by Freshfield, the first major summit to be attained by man was not Mt. Ararat after all. In the Caucasian version, while the Ark was drifting about in the flood waters, it first touched ground on the higher Elbrus before coming to rest on Ararat. The legend no doubt had less to do with a realistic assessment of the relative heights of the two mountains than with local pride.

▲ ATLAS MOUNTAINS ▲

The High Atlas extend eastward from the Atlantic coast of Morocco for over 300 miles, and are the highest, most extensive mountain range in North Africa. The highest portion, 40 miles south of Marrakech, is contained by the only two road passes over the range, the Tizi n Test on the west and the Tizi n Tichka on the east. These mountains form an impressive backdrop for Marrakech, especially in winter when the snow lies deep enough for good skiing and winter mountaineering. In summer the range is hot, dry, and barren, and climbing is not pleasant. The best time for hiking and mountaineering is the spring, since fall weather is somewhat stormier.

To approach Jebel Toubkal (13,655 feet), the highest summit, one takes the Marrakech-Taroudannt road for an hour to Asni, where there is a hotel and a youth hostel. From here, a dirt road runs 11 miles to the Berber village of Imlil (5600 feet), where there is a climber's hut and where muleteer-guides are available. The Neltner Hut, in the Mizane Valley just west of Jebel Toubkal at 10,500 feet, is a day's trek from Imlil. The normal route up Toubkal takes about four hours from the hut, and involves no technical difficulties.

Although most of the high summits can, like Jebel Toubkal, be climbed without rope, a number of peaks in the Toubkal region have tremendous walls, some offering over 2000 feet of difficult rock climbing. The most challenging include the south face of Angour, an 11,745-foot peak which is 15 miles northeast of Toubkal and just south of the ski area of Oukaimeden; the east face of Afella (13,265 feet), which faces Jebel Toubkal across the Mizane Valley; the west face of Biiguinnoussene (13,006 feet), north of Afella; and the north face of Tazarharht, perhaps the most impressive wall in the range. Oddly enough the summit of Tazarharht is a broad plateau. Good ridge climbs are found on 12,828-foot Aksoual, 12,773-foot Anrhemer, the Clocheton pinnacles (between Afella and Biiguinnoussene), and the west-southwest arete of Jebel Toubkal. In addition to the Imlil and Neltner huts, the Lepiney Hut and the Tacheddirt Hut are also important climbing bases; the former is at the foot of Tazarharht's north wall, and the latter lies between Angour on the north and Aksoual on the south.

For hikers, the trip from the Neltner Hut over 12,187-foot Tizi Ouanoums (Ouanoums Pass) to Lac d'Ifni, the only lake in the region, is very scenic. There are also trails over most of the other significant passes in the High Atlas. For

MAP 30. ATLAS MOUNTAINS

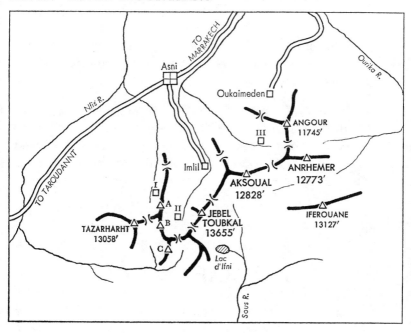

Peaks not Named

A   Biiguinnoussene 13006'

B   Afella 13265'

C   Ouanoukrim Sud 13416'

Huts not Named

I   Lepiney

II   Neltner

III   Tacheddirt

Scale 0   5   10 mi.

hikers interested in doing a little exploring, the country east of the Tizi n Tichka is a rarely visited wilderness with spectacular gorges. Skiers can choose the well-developed slopes at Oukaimeden, where a tow goes up to 10,000 feet, or they may prefer the fine cross-country skiing found in the High Atlas.

The High Atlas are but one of four Moroccan ranges that bear the name "Atlas." Southwest of the High Atlas are the Anti-Atlas, barren mountains which reach just under 8000 feet. The Middle Atlas are northeast of the High Atlas, and reach nearly 11,000 feet. The Rif Atlas (or Er Rif) parallel the Mediterranean coast and reach just over 8000 feet.

▲ SAHARA ▲

Mountains in the Sahara? Yes. In fact, there are startling rock peaks comparable to Shiprock and Agathla of our own desert southwest. Like these American monoliths, the most spectacular of the Saharan pinnacles are also volcanic plugs.

The highest mountain in the Sahara is 11,204-foot Emi Koussi, a broad volcanic cone in the Tibesti Mountains of northern Chad. Emi Koussi is an easy climb, but getting there is a bit of an adventure. From the airstrip at Gouro, 60 miles to the east, one travels by Land-Rover and camel to the base of the peak. Though Emi Koussi is a walk-up, elsewhere in the Tibesti there are innumerable sheer rock pinnacles waiting for their first challengers.

The Ahaggar mountains in southern Algeria are better known, more accessible, and even more spectacular than the Tibesti. In the Ahaggar one finds monoliths of truly mountainous proportions, of which perhaps the most magnificent is 7667-foot Garet el Djenoun, which is surrounded by sheer walls 1000 to 2000 feet high. The highest summit in the Ahaggar is 9574-foot Mt. Tahat, a huge heap of crumbled rock which is fatiguing but not technically difficult to climb. From the town of Tamanrasset, 35 miles south of the peak, there is a road to within about three miles of Tahat's summit. Ilamane (9050 feet), the second highest peak in the Ahaggar, has no unroped route up its precipitous sides.

Northeast of the Ahaggar is the Tassili-n-Ajjer (highest point 5814 feet), where one can find eroded sandstone formations reminiscent of Monument Valley. Other important mountain ranges in the Sahara include the Darfour Mountains in the western Sudan, which reach 10,131 feet in the volcanic Jebel Marra; the Air Mountains (highest point 5906 feet) in Niger; and the Jabal al 'Uweinat (6345 feet) near the junction of the boundaries of Egypt, Libya, and the Sudan.

The only reasonable time for climbing in the Sahara is November through April, but it can get very cold; on some midwinter days the temperature does not rise above freezing. There is occasionally a little snow on the highest peaks, but not enough to worry about. Summer is out for all normal human beings, since the daytime temperatures can soar to over 120°, although the nights are often quite cool. The high Tibesti has a reported diurnal range of nearly 100°.

▲ CAMEROON ▲

Mt. Cameroon, an active volcano so massive that it covers 700 square miles of the country of Cameroon, is the only big mountain in sub-Saharan West Africa. The mountain's 13,350-foot summit is just 14 miles from the Atlantic shore. In this century there have been major eruptions of Mt. Cameroon in 1909, 1922, 1954, and 1959; all of these consisted mainly of lava flows except the 1954 eruption, which deposited the ash and cinders that now cover the mountain's upper slopes.

The trail to the summit of Mt. Cameroon begins at Buea, five miles south of the summit at 3700 feet. Guides, porters, and provisions can be procured from the Mountain Hotel in Buea. After passing some farmlands, one enters a belt of rain forest which extends to about 7000 feet. Above that there are a few scattered trees to as high as 9000 feet, but for the most part the top 6000 feet of the mountain are grass covered. There are huts along the trail at 6000 feet, 9000 feet, and 13,250 feet; the last is still some 45 minutes from Fako Peak, the highest point on the mountain. Most hikers make the climb in two days, spending the night at the 9000-foot hut; however, this is a tough grind and three days are recommended.

Even more than most mountains, Mt. Cameroon creates

its own weather. Cold northeasterly winds sweep across the upper portion of the mountain and clash head-on with the moisture-laden warm air which moves inland from the sea. The result is torrential rainfall and incessant cloudiness. At Debundscha Point near the sea on the western slope of the mountain, the rainfall averages 400 inches a year, and meteorologists believe it is even greater higher up. The wettest months are June to October, and the driest November to March. But even during the latter period rain and fog are common, and it is almost always windy on the summit. One climber who made 10 ascents reported that he had a clear view only once, but on that occasion the wind was so strong that he could not enjoy it. The temperature on the summit regularly falls below freezing at night, and rarely gets much above that in the daytime. The ground not infrequently wears a thin mantle of snow. From the summit—when it is clear—one can see far inland to the pleasantly cool 8000-foot hills of the Cameroon Highlands. In the opposite direction, the mountainous island of Fernando Poo rises out of the ocean 50 miles away.

▲ SOUTH AFRICA & MALAWI ▲

South Africa

South Africa has no individual peaks to rival the giants of East Africa, but in the Drakensberg Mountains there is some of the finest mountain scenery on the continent. The range extends for 800 miles from Cape Province to the northern tip of Transvaal, but by far the most impressive section is that along the border between Natal and eastern Lesotho. The Lesotho side of the border is a high plateau which is cut off from the lowlands of Natal by one of the greatest escarpments on earth. This escarpment runs for a hundred miles and in places is as much as 4000 feet high. Some spectacular rock climbing has been done on the escarpment, but the rock is loose. Better rock climbing is found on the sandstone mountains of Cape Province, including 3567-foot Table Mountain, which rises above the streets of Cape Town.

The highest point in the Drakensberg, 11,425-foot Thabantshonyana, is a rather insignificant hill rising above the the Lesotho plateau, some miles back from the edge of the escarpment. The climb to the summit is easy, but long. The starting point is the Twin Streams Farm, which is 70 miles from Nottingham Road on the main Durban-Johannesburg highway. The climb takes about three days and involves an elevation gain of roughly 7000 feet. There is a trail up the Mohlesi Pass to the top of the escarpment.

Of greater interest from the climber's point of view are a number of impressive peaks along the edge of the escarpment. These include Champagne Castle (11,081 feet), Giants Castle (10,878 feet), Mont Aux Sources (10,769 feet), Cathkin Peak (10,438 feet), and Cathedral Peak (9856 feet). An interesting and popular climb is the Sentinel, a steep-sided peak in the Mont Aux Sources group in Royal Natal National Park; the ascent is a good tough scramble.

The Drakensberg can be climbed throughout the year, though in the high elevations there is some snowfall in winter, June to August. In summer there are fairly frequent thunder storms. There are some forests in the ravines at the lower elevations, but on the high plateau there are only shrubs and grass.

Climbers interested in more information on the mountains of South Africa can contact the Mountain Club of South Africa, P.O. Box 164, Cape Town.

Malawi

The highest mountains between the Drakensberg and the great volcanoes of East Africa are the spectacular rock domes of Mlanje Mountain in southern Malawi. The highest peak, 9847-foot Sapitwa, can be climbed in one very long day from the Likabula Forestry Depot, which is seven miles from the town of Mlanje, but it is more pleasant to make it in two days, staying overnight at a hut at about 6000 feet. There is a good trail much of the way, and the upper part of the route is marked by red arrows. Guides are not normally needed, but it should be possible to arrange for one through the Forester-Mlanje Mountain, P. O. Box 50, Mlanje, Malawi. Little rock climbing has been done on the peaks of Mlanje Mountain, but there is no doubt that challenging climbs could be found on their steep slopes of barren syenite and granite. Further information on Mlanje Mountain can be obtained from the Mlanje Mountain Club, P. O. Box 240, Blantyre.

▲ VIRUNGA MOUNTAINS ▲

The Virunga Mountains are a group of eight volcanoes which are shared by the Congo, Uganda, and Rwanda. The highest of the eight is the well-preserved cone of Karisimbi (14,782 feet), which is usually climbed in three days round trip from the west, starting at the village of Kibumba. The usual procedure is to hike on the first day to the 10,500-foot saddle between Karisimbi and 14,557-foot Mikeno, to climb the mountain on the second day, and to return to Kibumba on the third. (As of 1968, a hut near the saddle, the Kabara Hut, was not in usable condition. There is another hut, the Rukumi, at about 11,600 feet on the north slope of Karisimbi, and it may be in better shape.) Though an easy climb, Karisimbi was the scene of one of the worst accidents in the history

MAP 31. **VIRUNGA MOUNTAINS**

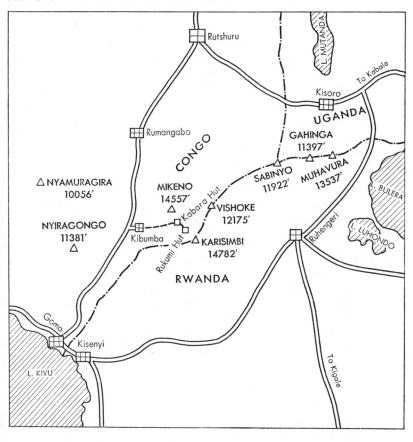

Border —·—

Scale 0   2   4   6   8   10 mi.

of mountaineering. In February 1907, the geologist Kirschstein and a caravan of lowland African porters were caught in a snow- and hail-storm high on the mountain and the porters, assuming the wrath of God was upon them, sat down to die. Although Kirschstein exhausted himself and caught pneumonia in the process of trying to drag the porters to safety, they refused to budge and 20 of them froze to death. Snow is not infrequent on the summit, but rarely lasts for more than a day or two.

The most interesting peak in the Virungas from the point of view of mountaineering is Mikeno, the precipitous eroded core of an old volcano. Mikeno defeated several attempts to climb it before the summit was finally reached in 1927. From the 10,500-foot saddle the summit can be reached in a steep scramble of about four hours. The wet, grass-covered slopes encountered en route are slippery and require considerable caution. The route skirts left of the steep rock wall which rises directly above the saddle.

The other six Virunga peaks are Muhavura (13,537 feet), Vishoke (12,175 feet), Sabinyo (11,922 feet), Gahinga (11,397 feet), Nyiragongo (11,381 feet), and Nyamuragira (10,056 feet). None are difficult to climb, though the rock pinnacles that form Sabinyo's serrated crest should offer some rock-climbing possibilities.

In the Virungas the upper limit of the forest is approximately 11,000 feet. From timberline to about 13,500 feet one finds the typical oversized plant life of the East African mountains, particularly giant senecios and lobelias. The Virunga Mountains are the habitat of the mountain gorilla, and it is conceivable that hikers may meet one on the trail.

According to George Schaller, whose study on the animal (*The Year of the Gorilla,* 1964) also gives a good description of the mountains, the best way to handle such encounters is to stand calmly and look the beast right in the eye—preferably from a distance. The gorilla looks fierce but is mild enough if not threatened. As far as is known, no climber has ever been harmed by one. Another source of information on the Virungas is Earl Denman's *Alone to Everest* (1954), the first part of which recounts his climbs of all eight Virunga peaks.

Although the Congo has gone through much political turmoil in recent years, the government has continued to maintain Albert National Park, through which the volcanoes are approached. Porters and guides should still be available at Kibumba, though climbers should try to confirm this in advance if possible.

▲ RUWENZORI ▲

No mountains have a more interesting history of discovery and exploration than the Ruwenzori Mountains on the Congo-Uganda border. Although their very existence was not confirmed until H. M. Stanley's expedition sighted them in 1888, man's interest in the range can be said to have begun in the second century A.D., when the geographer Ptolemy drew on his map of Africa a range of mountains which he named the "Mountains of the Moon"; these he placed where he thought the headwaters of the Nile should be. The peaks we know today as the Ruwenzori, whose snows do feed the Nile, lie just where Ptolemy placed his mountains. From Ptolemy's day until 1888, the "Mountains of the Moon" appeared again and again on maps, but the later cartographers were just copying from Ptolemy; there is no record of any European actually having seen the Ruwenzori. Even Ptolemy's ultimate source is uncertain, though it has been speculated that he got his information from the Sabaean Arabs. Perhaps his belief in snow mountains in equatorial Africa was strengthened by reports of the mountains of Ethiopia or of the snows of Kilimanjaro, which could have been spotted from near the East African coast by contemporary Greek travelers.

Whatever the source of Ptolemy's surmise may have been, by the time Africa began to be explored in the 19th century the discovery of the mysterious "Mountains of the Moon" had become perhaps the most sought-after explorer's prize on the continent. The accepted name of the range is "Ruwenzori" meaning "place whence come the rains," but to many people they are still the "Mountains of the Moon."

Stanley's distant view did not remove the mystery from the Ruwenzori. They were still surrounded by miles of impenetrable jungle and enshrouded in almost perpetual mist. The effort to reach the high inner portion of the range began very soon after Stanley filed his report, but there were a total of 23 expeditions before the Italian Duke of Abruzzi finally succeeded in reaching the major summits in 1906.

Thanks to efficient organization and good luck with the weather, the Duke's expedition succeeded in climbing the

MAP 32. RUWENZORI

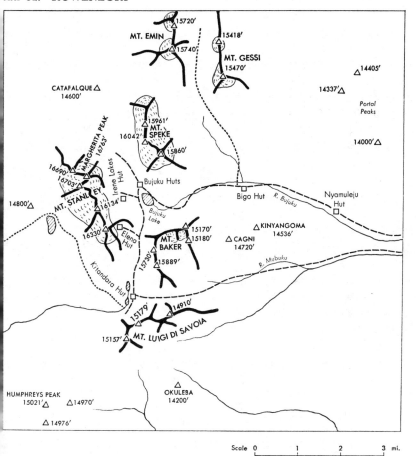

MT. EMIN
15720'
15740'

15418'
MT. GESSI
15470'

△14405'

14337'△

Portal
Peaks

CATAFALQUE △
14600'

14000'△

MT.
SPEKE
15961'
16042'
15860'

MARGHERITA PEAK
16763'
16690'
16703'

MT. STANLEY
16134'

14800'△

16330'

Irene Lakes
Hut

Bujuku Huts

Bujuku
Lake

Elena
Hut

MT.
BAKER
15170'
15180'

15230'

15889'

Bigo Hut

R. Bujuku

Nyamuleju
Hut

△ KINYANGOMA
14536'

△ CAGNI
14720'

R. Mubuku

Kitandara Hut

15179

14910'

15157'△ MT. LUIGI DI SAVOIA

HUMPHREYS PEAK
15021'△   △14970'

△ 14976'

△
OKULEBA
14200'

Scale 0   1   2   3 mi.

six highest mountains in the range, in addition to making a very thorough scientific and cartographic study. The Duke had a staff of professional guides and scientists, and over 200 local porters. This was one of the first really large-scale mountaineering expeditions, and it contributed much knowledge and experience to the expeditions that soon began to explore the Himalayas. Mountaineers were so overwhelmed by the Duke of Abruzzi's triumph that they felt for a long time that there was little more to be done in the Ruwenzori. It was 20 years before the Englishman G. N Humphreys made the second successful expedition. Second ascents do not win many accolades but Humphreys deserves high marks for spunk. On one climb after falling into a crevasse and breaking an arm, he instructed his inexperienced companion in step-cutting, and then proceeded to the summit.

In area the Ruwenzori is not large; it is only some 60 miles north-south, by 30 miles east-west. Like the Snow Mountains of New Guinea and the Sierra Nevada de Cocuy of Colombia the Ruwenzori are an arctic island rising directly from a tropical base; in all three ranges the meeting of warm air and cold heights makes for almost perpetual mist. The snow-line in the Ruwenzori is about 15,000 feet.

Above 10,000 feet elevation in the Ruwenzori there is one of the most luxuriant rain forests on earth. Ordinary plants grow to tree size, and are covered with moss. Everything is constantly wet and portions of even the best trails become slimy bogs; other sections are dim-lit tunnels under a thick canopy of vegetation. Only the main trail up the Mobuku and Bujuku valleys to Lake Bujuku is kept open; for any walking away from this trail bushwacking is likely necessary.

Lake Bujuku (13,000 feet) is the main climbing base for the high peaks. It is generally reached in three day's walking from the end of the road at Nyakalengija; the trip can be made in two very long days, but the huts are not conveniently spaced for this. The first night is usually spent at the Nyabitaba Hut (8700 feet), and the second at either the Nyamuleju Hut (10,900 feet) of the Bigo Hut (11,300 feet). At Lake Bujuku (actually some 15 minutes above the lake) there are two huts. Climbers planning to use any of these huts should make local arrangements to reserve space and to obtain the keys to the huts, as the huts do tend to become crowded during the climbing season. This procedure must be followed or climbers may arrive at the huts to find themselves locked out.

In the Ruwenzori there are six mountains which rise to over 15,000 feet and carry glaciers: Stanley (16,763), Speke (16,042), Baker (15,889), Emin (15,740), Gessi (15,470), and Luigi di Savoia (15,179). Mt. Stanley is a broad glacier-covered mountain which offers no easy way up. On every route there is technical climbing on either rock or ice or both, but perhaps the greatest danger to the inexperienced is the risk of getting lost in the mist. There is no "normal" route up Stanley and there is some debate as to which is the easiest, because the difficulty of the routes varies under different snow conditions. Sometimes there are large cornices, and then otherwise relatively easy ridges become treacherous. Experienced local climbers suggest that on the average the east-ridge route offers the least difficulty, partly because as a ridge it is easier to follow in the mist; also it is less corniced than some of the other ridges. The route starts from the Irene Lakes Hut (at 14,750 feet), a two-and-a-half hour walk from the

Bujuku Huts. From the Irene Lakes one walks north to the foot of the stony gully at about the same elevation as the lakes, then scrambles up it to the crest of the ridge. There is one "rock step" which has two pitches of rather difficult climbing, but aside from that the ridge involves only moderately difficult technical climbing. It is of course no place for inexperienced climbers.

Mt. Speke is easier than Stanley and is the usual goal of moderately experienced parties. It can be climbed by strong hikers, but only with an experienced leader and proper equipment. As with Mt. Stanley, one of the main difficulties is route finding when it is misty. The normal route up Victor Emmanuel Peak (the highest point on Speke) is via its southwest ridge and the Speke Glacier; the ridge begins near Stuhlmann Pass, which is above the Bujuku Huts. There is a guidebook to the entire range—*A Guide to the Ruwenzori,* by H. A. Osmaston and D. Pasteur—which describes routes up all the major Ruwenzori peaks in detail.

Porters belonging to the local Bakonjo tribe can be booked; bookings should be made at least two weeks in advance. In addition to the ordinary porters a headman should be hired. He will probably speak a little English and will be responsible for organizing the work of the porters. The porters do not generally wear shoes, and are therefore limited to regions below the snowline. Many can and will go higher, but the visitors must supply the boots and socks and if necessary the crampons. The headman can be relied on to know the routes to all the huts and major points below the snowline, but not necessarily the routes up the peaks. Some headmen do know the route up Speke, however, and if one of them is needed, this should be specified when making arrangements for the porters. Aside from this there are no guides available for Ruwenzori climbs, which means that climbers must either be experienced enough to get along without them or else make arrangements with climbers or guides who know the range.

There are two relatively dry seasons—from early December to mid-March, and from early June to early September. During these periods precipitation is not excessive though there is still much mist which often lasts all day. But in a week's stay at the Bujuku Huts during the "dry" seasons, there will usually be at least a few clear moments at dawn or dusk and occasionally even during midday. During the rest of the year no one in his right mind climbs in the Ruwenzori.

▲ TANZANIA ▲

Kilimanjaro

Kilimanjaro rises in complete isolation from a plain varying between 3000 and 5000 feet elevation to a height of 19,340 feet. The mountain has two peaks: the higher is Kibo, which wears the broad, nearly flat white cap so often seen in photographs of the wildlife of the Amboseli Game Reserve; six miles east of Kibo, and separated from it by a broad, 14,500-foot-high saddle, is Mawenzi (16,890 feet), the eroded core of an older volcano. From a distance Kibo's huge cone dominates the horizon, and Mawenzi looks like a mere formless hump; but from closer up Mawenzi turns out to be a rugged group of rock spires. Technical climbers who go to Kilimanjaro spend most of their time on Mawenzi.

Perhaps no other mountain on earth is as visible as Kilimanjaro, which has a base roughly 30 miles north-to-south by 50 miles east-to-west. It has been seen from the Indian Ocean, 160 miles away, and even from Mt. Kenya, 200 miles to the north. When the mountain is seen from far out on the plains, the East African haze often blots out the lower slopes and Kibo's icecap floats cloudlike high above the horizon. The summit of Kibo is an ice-filled caldera one-and-a-half miles across, with a rim varying in elevation from 18,600 to 19,340 feet. Within the caldera there is a smaller, more recent crater 370 yards in diameter.

Kilimanjaro is encircled by a forest belt lying between roughly 6200 feet and 9800 feet elevation. In general the forest is not as dense as that of Mt. Kenya, much less the Ruwenzori, but on the south side there is a genuine rain forest. Above timberline the typical high-altitude African flora—giant groundsel, lobelias, etc.—extends to 14,000 feet. The glaciers which descend from Kibo's summit icecap reach down in one place to just above 15,000 feet.

The German geographer Hans Meyer was the first to reach

Kibo's summit region when in 1887 he made a determined effort which ultimately took him to around 18,000 feet. Upon returning Meyer claimed to have reached the summit, but the account he wrote left too many questions unanswered, and certain perceptive mountaineers became convinced that he had not reached the top at all. Meyer reconsidered his claim and admitted he might have been mistaken. Then, swallowing his pride, he showed rare courage for someone whose honor has been besmirched, and in 1889 he returned to Africa with Austrian guide Ludwig Purtscheller to win legitimately the honor of making the first ascent of the continent's highest mountain.

Now Kibo is climbed yearly by hundreds of people, and it is the highest mountain on earth that has what can be called a "tourist route." For many tourists with no mountaineering experience but lots of stamina, Kibo has been the very first mountain climb. On the other hand, no small number of quite competent Alpinists have ground to a halt, gasping for breath, on the steep scree slopes above 15,000 feet. The "tourist route" is 70 miles round trip, takes five days, and has a total altitude gain of almost 15,000 feet. Though there are no technical difficulties, this is indeed no small undertaking. For snow and ice climbers a number of technical routes can also be found on Kibo.

The "tourist route" begins at Marangu, at 4600 feet on the south slope of the mountain. Marangu is reached by a good road from Moshi and has two hotels, the Marangu and the Kibo, which specialize in organizing hiking safaris to the summit. The all-inclusive tour is reasonably priced and highly recommended, as it gives one the feeling of being on a real

MAP 33. **KILIMANJARO**, Tanzania

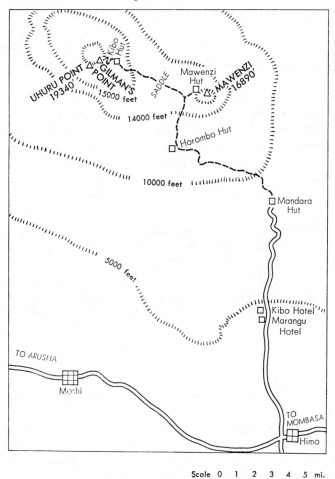

Kibo Hut

UHURU POINT
19340

GILMAN'S POINT
15000 feet

SADDLE

Mawenzi Hut

MAWENZI
16890

14000 feet

Horombo Hut

10000 feet

Mandara Hut

5000 feet

Kibo Hotel

Marangu Hotel

TO ARUSHA

Moshi

TO MOMBASA

Himo

Scale 0 1 2 3 4 5 mi.

African safari, as well as leaving nothing to think about but climbing those 15,000 vertical feet. The tour includes guides, porters, meals, bedding, and assured accommodations in the huts en route. There is much to be said for doing it yourself in the mountains, but if a climber is ever going to indulge in a bit of luxury, this is a good place to do it.

From Marangu a four-wheel-drive vehicle road leads 11 miles to the first hut (Mandara; formerly named Bismarck) at 9000 feet. One can, of course, drive this portion, but long experience has shown that taking a day to walk it is an excellent way to begin the slow conditioning and acclimatization that are needed for success three days later. The first half of the route to Mandara Hut is through heavily populated farmland, while the last half penetrates the virtually uninhabited rain forest. From Mandara Hut the trail continues another 11 miles to Horombo Hut (formerly named Peter's Hut), at 12,000 feet, where the second night is spent. The third day is a 10-mile walk to Kibo Hut (15,420 feet), just below the final slopes of Kibo. Kibo Hut is as high as most tourists are ever likely to spend the night, and at this altitude the heart pumps relentlessly and the temples throb; most people get little if any sleep. The next morning parties set off at 1:00 or 2:00 A.M. and begin the 3200-foot climb up the steep scree slopes to Gilman's Point (18,635 feet) on the rim of the caldera. From here the summit is still over a mile away and 700 feet higher; it is reached by following the rim clockwise. At times the snow on the rim makes crampons necessary, and climbers should ask about snow conditions before setting out. On the descent the usual procedure is to go all the way down to Horombo Hut on the same day as the summit climb, and to return back to Marangu on the following (i.e., fifth) day.

Kibo can be climbed any time of the year, but the driest and best climbing months are August through October. March through May, and November through December, are the rainy seasons, and the rain on the lower slopes and snow above 14,000 feet alter the nature of the climb considerably.

There is no walking route up Mawenzi, though the highest point, Hans Meyer Peak, can be climbed by routes involving only moderately difficult roped rock climbing. Mawenzi should not be attempted by inexperienced climbers except under expert leadership.

Other Mountains in Tanzania

Forty miles west-southwest of Kilimanjaro is another volcano, Mt. Meru (14,979 feet), which would attract wider notice were it not overshadowed by its giant neighbor. Meru, which rises directly above the town of Arusha, can be climbed in two days from Olkokola (about 8000 feet), where guides and porters can usually be procured. There is a hut on the upper slopes of the mountain. The east side of Meru's cone appears to have been blasted away in an eruption and that face of the mountain is now a 3000-foot-high cliff.

The Kipengere Range just north of Lake Nyasa reaches 9713 feet in Rungwe Mountain, the highest point in southern Tanzania.

▲ KENYA ▲

To most tourists the mountain that symbolizes Africa is Kilimanjaro, but to climbers the continent's most interesting mountain is Mt. Kenya. The startling form of this 17,058-foot giant invites comparison with the Matterhorn or Ushba, while its majestic isolation puts it in a class with Kilimanjaro or Ararat. Mt. Kenya well deserves the distinction of being the only mountain in the world to have given its name to an entire country.

Mt. Kenya's base (at roughly 5000 feet elevation) is even broader than that of Kilimanjaro, and even at the 11,000-foot contour the mountain covers some 150 square miles. From the massive proportions of this lower portion of the mountain, geologists have estimated that a million years ago the original Kibo-like rounded form of Mt. Kenya reached 23,000 feet—4000 feet higher than Kilimanjaro, and higher than any volcano extant today. Today Mt. Kenya's slopes climb gradually to about 15,000 feet, but the final 2000 feet leap upward in tremendous precipices.

The first ascent of Mt. Kenya was made in 1899 by the British geographer Sir Halford Mackinder and the two Italian guides Cesar Ollier and Joseph Brocherel. Mackinder is one of the rare figures in mountaineering history who is

MAP 34.   MT. KENYA, KENYA

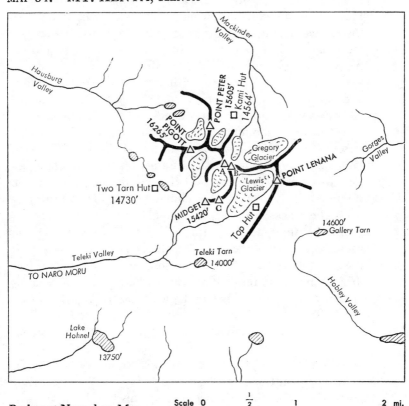

Peaks not Named on Map

A   Batian 17058′

B   Nelion 17022′

C   Point John 16020′

remembered primarily for his achievements in another field. He was not an experienced mountaineer, and he undertook the Kenya ascent more for geographic exploration than for mountaineering. Departing from Nairobi, Mackinder's party of six Europeans and 164 Africans took a month to reach the mountain. En route they were attacked by rhinos and more than one hostile tribe, and one engagement left two African members of the party dead. Surely Mackinder's was one of very few mountaineering expeditions to suffer combat losses. After establishing a base camp at 10,300 feet, the party launched several unsuccessful assaults on the mountain before Mackinder and the two Italians finally reached the summit. Mt. Kenya was not climbed again for 30 years.

Of the tracks which approach Mt. Kenya from various directions, the quickest route to Top Hut (15,530 feet), the usual base for summit climbs, is the Naro Moru track from the west. Depending on the season, sedans or four-wheel-drive vehicles can reach 10,000 feet, where there is a clearing known as the "Met (meteorological) Clearing" where cars can be left. It is about an 11-hour walk from there to Top Hut. Top Hut is situated just across the Lewis Glacier from the great southeast face of Nelion (17,022 feet), which is the lower of Mt. Kenya's two hornlike summits; Nelion is 150 yards east-southeast of 17,058-foot Batian. The so-called normal route up Mt. Kenya goes up this face by a series of chimneys and ledges, then over the top of Nelion and across the connecting ridge to Batian. Though the term "normal route" is innocuous enough, novices should not be misled into thinking it is for them. There is no nontechnical route up Mt. Kenya, and even the easiest route involves rather difficult rock and ice climbing. The summit of Kenya can be reached only by strong climbers under expert leadership. For such climbers the average time from Top Hut to Batian is just over six hours. This and other routes are described in detail in the excellent *Guidebook to Mount Kenya and Kilimanjaro,* published by the Mountain Club of Kenya, P. O. Box 5741, Nairobi.

With the great rock walls of Batian and Nelion plus many lower pinnacles, the rock-climbing possibilities on Mt. Kenya are virtually limitless. The rock is loose in places, but for the most part firm enough for good climbing. It is considerably firmer than that of Mawenzi—Kilimanjaro's second summit —which like Kenya is an eroded volcanic cone. For tourists out to enjoy a mountain hike, Mt. Kenya's summit is clearly beyond reach, but there are numerous possibilities for walking and scrambling in the vast expanse of high country above the forest zone. After Batian and Nelion, the highest significant summit is 16,355-foot Point Lenana, which is about one kilometer east of Nelion. From Top Hut, Lenana can be reached with little difficulty in about an hour via its southwest ridge. Near the top, where one must move onto the edge of the Lewis Glacier, it is sometimes necessary to cut steps, but usually steps can be kicked in the snow. Lenana's summit provides a spectacular view of the southeast face of Nelion.

The forest belt on Mt. Kenya is between roughly 7000 and 11,000 feet. Below the forest is the typical East African savanna, while above it is a grassland zone which has the same type of oversized plantlife that one finds in the Ruwenzori, though on a lesser scale. Giant groundsel and lobelias, which are the most common of these plants, extend up to about

14,000 feet. The permanent snowline is at a little over 15,000 feet, and 12 small glaciers cling to the precipitous upper slopes. The Lewis Glacier covers about one-square kilometer and contains half the total ice on the mountain.

Kenya has two rainy seasons—from mid-March to late June, and from mid-October to late December—and the peak receives much snow during these periods. The best weather is usually from mid-January to late February and from late August through September. Even during the dry periods it often clouds up in the afternoon, though three or four hours of clear weather can usually be counted on in the morning.

Visitors to Mt. Kenya would be well advised to make contact with the Mountain Club of Kenya, which can provide information on transportation, porters, equipment, and guides. Although the summit of Mt. Kenya was reached as early as 1959 by an African climber, there are as yet no African guides; however, a couple of local firms offer deluxe safaris up the mountain which include competent European guides.

Other Mountains in Kenya

Mt. Elgon, on the Uganda-Kenya border, is a massive volcano which can be climbed from either country. From the Uganda side it is a two-day hike from Bumagabula (5500 feet). On the Kenya side a road passable for sedans in the dry season leads from Kitale, through Endebess, to 10,000 feet elevation, from where the climb can be done in one day. The crater rim of Elgon is about five miles in diameter; the highest point—14,178-foot Wagagai—is in Uganda, while the highest point on the Kenyan portion of the rim is 14,112 feet. There is a hut operated by the Uganda Mountain Club on the floor of the crater at 12,500 feet. Guides are available locally for either approach.

Just 50 miles west of Mt. Kenya are the Aberdare Mountains, which reach 13,120 feet in Mt. Satima. Not spectacular as mountains go, the range consists mainly of a delightfully cool 10,000-foot-high moorland plateau topped by a number of large hills. Satima can be climbed in an easy day from the end of Land-Rover tracks on the north or east; or it can be climbed from the south in a long day from near the crest of the east-west road across Aberdare National Park. Satima presents no technical difficulties, but there are route-finding problems; information on guides can be obtained in Nyeri or through the Mountain Club of Kenya.

▲ ETHIOPIA ▲

Central Ethiopia is a high plateau that has a pleasant climate throughout the year, with the exception of two short rainy seasons. The capital of the country, Addis Ababa, lies at 8000 feet, and few portions of the plateau are much below this elevation. The edges of the plateau drop abruptly, particularly in the east where within a few miles there is a drop of 8000 feet to the scorching lowlands along the Red Sea. The highest of the many mountain groups which rise above the general level of the plateau are the Semyen Mountains in the northern part of the country, northeast of Gondar.

Africa is known for its great escarpments, of which one of the most impressive is that on the northwest side of the Semyen. This escarpment is over 20 miles long and rises in a series of steps to a height of 4000 feet above its base. Geologically, the Semyen Mountains are the eroded remnants of a vast shield volcano. The present topography is the result of the tilting of the original surface upward toward the northwest, where faulting originally formed the escarpment, followed by erosion which dug deep, roughly parallel valleys that drain toward the southeast. Thus, the mountains we find today are long ridges ("hogbacks") which slope gently upward to summits near the edge of the escarpment. All the major peaks offer easy routes up their south slopes.

The ascent of Ras Dashan (15,158 feet), the highest peak in Ethiopia, is not technically difficult, but is a real adventure. The road from Axum to Gondar skirts the western edge of the Semyen and comes within 30 airline miles of Ras Dashan at the town of Debarek (about 9000 feet), from where a trail leads to the peak. The trek to the summit takes about a week round trip. From Debarek, the trail heads northeast near the crest of the escarpment to the village of Geech (about 10,500 feet), which is reached in something less than two full days. The section of the escarpment near Geech is the last remaining habitat of the Walia Ibex, a sure-footed wild goat. A national park has been established to protect the 150 or so animals that remain (as of 1968), and hopefully their numbers will increase.

MAP 35. RAS DASHAN, ETHIOPIA

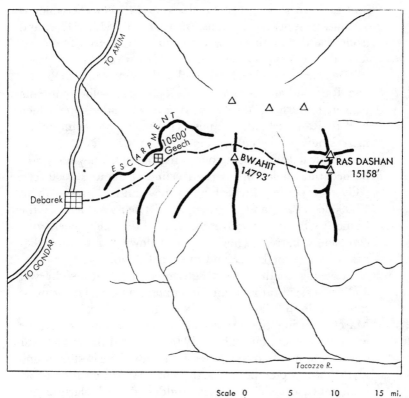

From Geech one continues eastward to the Bwahit Pass on the northern slopes of Mt. Bwahit (14,793 feet), which is 10 miles west of Ras Dashan. The pass is over 13,000 feet and from it the summit of Bwahit is an easy climb. (There are several other peaks in the Semyen which are over 14,000 feet.)

The track across the cultivated valley between Mt. Bwahit and Ras Dashan drops to about 8600 feet before climbing back up to the final 2000 feet of scree and boulder slopes which lead to Ras Dashan's summit. This valley has come under increasingly heavy cultivation in recent decades by farmers who know nothing about conserving the soil. They have now pushed their fields up to the treeline at about 12,000 feet, while their cattle graze as high as they can find grass—about 13,000 feet. After a few years there will be no soil left and the farmers will have to move on, leaving this once green area completely barren. They will be following a pattern that has been repeated over and over in Ethiopia.

Traveling conditions in the Semyen are affected by wet and dry seasons rather than winter and summer. The heaviest rains are in July and August and the "small rains" are in March. During the heavy rains, hail or snow sometimes whitens the mountains above 12,000 feet and the trails lower down become almost impassably muddy. The best climbing months are September through February, but even then fog, rain, snow, or hail may occur suddenly, particularly in the afternoon. Parties should therefore be properly equipped for high altitude weather.

For climbers in the Semyen, the town of Gondar has the closest hotel, auto repair, and other facilities, and is the administrative center of the region. Muleteers and guides can be procured in Debarek, or by writing in advance to the Game Warden, Semyen Mountain National Park, P. O. Box 13, Gondar; English-speaking guides are available. Travel in the Semyen should become easier in the next few years since tourist facilities are being developed in the national park. A road currently under construction will considerably shorten the trek to Geech.

Very little rock climbing has been done in the Semyen, partly because the rock is not good. However, for climbers who do not object to friable basaltic rock, there are a number of very impressive spires which are detached from the escarpment, and which have never been climbed. An intriguing goal for rock climbers would be Princes Rock, near Gondar. There was once a prison on top where prisoners of royal blood were kept. A track went to the summit and ruins can still be seen there, but the track has since disappeared, leaving the ruins isolated atop this unusual rock-climber's pinnacle.

Outside of the Semyen, probably the only other peak in Ethiopia over 14,000 feet is Batu (14,131) in the Mendebo Mountains, 150 miles south-southeast of Addis Ababa. Elsewhere in the country there are many peaks over 12,000 feet, and one could almost certainly still find first ascents among them.

▲ MADAGASCAR & REUNION ▲

Malagasy Republic (Madagascar)

Several groups of mountains rise above the plateau that occupies the interior of the Malagasy Republic, the world's largest one-island nation. The highest peak is Maromokotro (9436 feet) in the volcanic Massif du Tsaratanana, which is located in a remote region near the northern tip of the island. The shortest approach to the mountain is from the south, where the starting point is the village of Mangindrano (3560 feet). During the dry season, August through October, the village can be reached by road from the town of Bealanana. From Mangindrano, which is about 22 miles from the peak, the trail to the top takes three or four days round trip. Guides and porters can be hired at the village. There is a somewhat longer approach to Maromokotro from the west, where the starting point is the village of Marovato, which is reached by road from Ambanja.

The second highest peak on the island is 8720-foot Pic Boby in the granitic Andringitra massif, where there are rock faces and towers which would be of interest to technical climbers. Andringitra is 230 miles south of Tananarive, the pleasantly cool capital city of the republic. Just 40 miles south of Tananarive is the island's third highest peak, 8671-foot Ankaratra, which is easily accessible.

Reunion

The highest mountain in the Indian Ocean is the volcano Piton des Neiges (10,069 feet) on the island of Reunion. The original form of the mountain has been eroded into three steep-sided semicircular basins (called "cirques") and the ridges that separate them. The summit is the hub of these ridges. The starting point for the trail to the summit of Piton des Neiges is the mountain resort of Cilaos (4000 feet), in the Cirque de Cilaos on the south side of the peak. Cilaos has several hotels, and guides and porters can be procured there. The usual procedure is to climb the peak in two days, spending the night at the Caverne Dufourg Hut at 7500 feet. The trail is good but steep. The upper limit of forest is approximately 6000 feet. The best time for climbing is the winter, May through October, which is the dry season; snow falls occasionally on the summit, but melts away rapidly.

Reunion has another volcano, 7746-foot Piton de la Fournaise, which is still quite active; its summit is a two-day round-trip hike from Nez de Boeuf.

▲ ARABIAN PENINSULA ▲

Classical writers compared Yemen with the rest of the Arabian peninsula and called it "Arabia Felix"—Happy Arabia. In contrast to the scorching desert that occupies most of the vast peninsula, the mountains of Yemen are indeed an oasis of pleasant climate, relatively plentiful rainfall, and comparatively verdant valleys. Yemen is the most densely populated section of Arabia and the only sizable area in which the nomad life gives way to farming.

The mountains of Yemen are cultivated up to about 9000 feet and are noted for their remarkable terracing, which rivals that of Luzon in the Philippines. Some of these well-constructed and well-maintained terraces are many hundreds of years old. One of the most interesting sights in Yemen is a mountain named Jabal Sabir (9863 feet), which rises 5000 feet above the city of Taizz, and which is elaborately terraced almost all the way to its summit. Mountaineering archaeologists will be interested to note that the remains of pre-Islamic buildings have been found on many summits in Yemen.

Sana, the capital city of Yemen, is pleasantly situated at an elevation of 7900 feet, and is surrounded by mountains several thousand feet higher. The highest peak in Yemen and in the whole peninsula is probably 12,336-foot Jabal Hadur

Nabi Shuayb (or Jabal Hadur), about 20 miles southwest of Sana. The mountain is not difficult of access, as it is located just north of the highway that connects Sana with the port city of Hodeida. In north-central Yemen there are summits which rival Jabal Hadur in height.

Outside of Yemen, the highest summits on the peninsula are in the Jabal al Akhdar (10,400-foot Jabal ash Sham) in Oman, and the Jabal al Hijaz (10,279-foot Jabal Sawda), which is in Saudi Arabia just north of the Yemen border.

▲ SINAI ▲

If we must discount Noah's journey to the top of Mt. Ararat on the grounds that he did not get there under his own steam, then the credit for the first ascent of a major mountain goes to Moses for his assault on Mt. Sinai. Today Sinai remains a mountain well worth visiting, not only for its historical association, but also because it is an imposing peak in an intriguing wilderness of barren rock mountains.

To reach Mt. Sinai, one can drive on a four-wheel-drive vehicle road from Abu Rudeis on the west coast of the Sinai Peninsula, to 1400-year-old St. Catherine's Monastery, at 5000 feet on the north side of the mountain. Accommodations are available at both Abu Rudeis and St. Catherine's Monastery. From the monastery to the 7497-foot summit there is a path of 3000 stone steps, which have been trod over the centuries by tens of thousands of pilgrims.

Actually, Mt. Sinai itself is not the highest point in the massif. Mt. Katerina (8652 feet), two miles southwest of Sinai, claims that distinction. The small chapel on the summit of Mt. Katerina can be reached by a path from the top of Sinai. The two mountains can be climbed any time of year, but in winter climbers should be prepared for subfreezing temperatures.

▲ LEBANON ▲

Lebanon is a small country, only one-fourth the size of Switzerland, but it is a country of big mountains. The highest peak, 10,131-foot Qurnat as Sawda, is in the Lebanon Range which runs north and south down the center of the country. Along the Lebanon-Syria border is another major range. Its northern section is called the Anti-Lebanon and reaches 8625 feet; the southern part consists of the massif of Mt. Hermon (9232 feet).

The ascent of Qurnat as Sawda is an easy hike up the south side from the Cedars of Lebanon, at about 6000 feet. With several hundred trees, the Cedars of Lebanon is the last remaining grove of the magnificent cedar forests which once covered the range. The name Lebanon means "white as milk" in ancient Aramaic, and the higher summits of the Lebanon Range are white with snow a good half of the year. The lower limit of snowfall is about 2000 feet elevation. Skiing is a popular sport, with well-developed facilities.

The gentle, treeless slopes of Mt. Hermon can be ascended in one day from the Lebanese side. Mt. Hermon has been the goal of worshipers since even before its association with the transfiguration of Christ, and hikers with an interest in archaeology will find the ruins of a number of ancient temples high on the slopes of this massive mountain.

▲ TURKEY ▲

Mt. Ararat

"The earliest mountain ascent of which any record has been preserved is the ascent of Mt. Ararat by the patriarch Noah. It was accomplished in a combination of circumstances which is exceedingly unlikely to recur, and scarcely falls within the scope of the present inquiry." Thus begins Francis Gribble's comprehensive history of mountaineering, *The Early Mountaineers* (1899). Credit for the first ascent of Ararat in modern times—using the more conventional mountaineering technique of walking—goes to the German Dr. Frederic Parrot, who reached the summit in 1829. In 1876 James Bryce, who once served as British ambassador to the U.S., made what was probably the third ascent, the second having been that of a Russian general in charge of a topographic survey in 1850. Bryce's expedition was marked by a moment of excitement when at 13,000 feet, well above timberline and far above the range of local herders, he came upon a block of wood some four feet long and five inches thick. Could this be part of Noah's Ark? Bryce darted toward it "with a glee that astonished" his two companions, a Cossack and a Kurd, but he was finally forced to conclude that the block was probably not part of the Ark after all. His account did not go into the prosaic details, but reading between the lines we can guess that the block had been left by the Russian surveyors. In the late 1940's there was a worldwide flurry of interest when an American airman reported seeing what looked like the outline of an ark near Ararat's summit; however, despite the fact that the mountain has been climbed many times in recent years, no one has found anything more hopeful than Ambassador Bryce's chunk of wood.

Mt. Ararat is one of the most impressive volcanoes on earth. It rises 14,000 feet above the plain of the Aras River, which forms the Russian-Turkish border only 20 miles to the northeast. It stands in almost complete isolation and is visible for over 100 miles in all directions. The only mountain in the vicinity that even begins to rival Ararat's 16,916-foot-high summit is Little Ararat (12,877 feet), a Fuji-like cone about 10 miles to the southeast which is joined to the main peak by a saddle over 8000 feet high.

There are two possible bases for climbing to the summit of Ararat, one on the north (Aralik) and one on the south (Dogubayazit). The more frequently used is Dogubayazit, which

MAP 36. MT. ARARAT, TURKEY

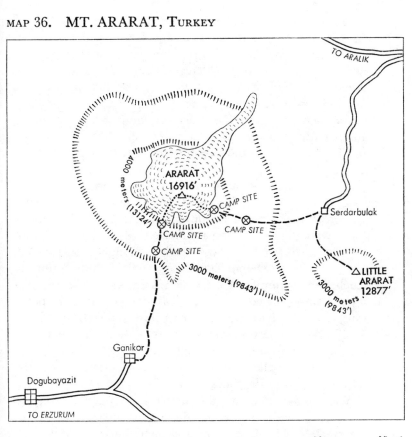

TO ARALIK

ARARAT
16916'

4000 meters (13124')

CAMP SITE

CAMP SITE

CAMP SITE

CAMP SITE

Serdarbulak

LITTLE
ARARAT
12877'

3000 meters (9843')

3000 meters
(9843')

Ganikor

Dogubayazit

TO ERZURUM

Scale 0   5   10   15 mi.

is on one of the main highways in eastern Turkey. Here climbers can find hotels, restaurants, and stores, and can make arrangements for guides and packhorses. From Dogubayazit cars can be driven to the village of Ganikor, where the trail begins. The trail heads north for seven or eight hours past small villages and nomad camps to a plateau at 10,500 feet, where there is a camp site. One can camp either here or at another camp site at 13,000 feet. The climb to the summit can be done in two days round trip, but most people take three.

Above the higher camp site the route is up a cinder and rock ridge which is just west of an impressive hanging glacier. This glacier reaches down to about 13,000 feet, and is the lowest glacier on the southern side of the mountain, though on the northeast side one glacial tongue reaches down somewhat lower. The cinder and rock ridge is followed until one reaches the summit glacier, which is crevassed and requires rope, crampons, and ice axe. At least one person in the party must be qualified to lead on ice, or a guide should be hired. For ice climbers interesting routes are easy to find. The view from the summit of Ararat is one of the most extensive on earth, and on a clear day the Caucasus Mountains stretch across the northern horizon 150 miles away.

Ararat is in dry country and with the exception of one area of birch forest on the north side of Little Ararat the slopes are treeless. The best months for climbing are July and August, when the chances are good for a clear view from the summit; however, even then there may be some cloudiness and precipitation by midafternoon.

Other Mountains in Turkey

Mt. Ararat is certainly Turkey's most imposing mountain, but there are also many other mountains of great interest in the country. The second highest peak, 14,457-foot Suphan Dagi, is a volcano which rises 9000 feet above the shores of Lake Van. It is a three-day climb from Adilcevay.

The third highest peak, 13,675-foot Gelyasin (also known as Resko), is in the Cilo-Sat Mountains in the southeastern corner of Turkey. This surprisingly alpine region just north of the Iraqi border contains steep rock peaks and over 20 glaciers. Gelyasin can be climbed in three days from the Zap Police Station, which is west of the mountain and 140 miles south of Van by a good road. A nontechnical route can be found up the east side of Gelyasin, but the route is complicated and one should take a rope. The west face of Gelyasin is one of the most impressive rock walls in Turkey. Guides can be found in the town of Hakkari, 10 miles south of Zap, but they cannot be counted on to be technically proficient. The Cilo-Sat peaks can also be approached in about the same amount of time from the east, where the village of Yuksekova is the take-off point.

Another range of very alpine mountains is the Rize Kackar, which is parallel to the Black Sea coastline in northeast Turkey. Kackar Peak (12,917 feet), the highest in the range, is a two-day climb round trip from the Ayder hot springs. The upper portion of the route ascends the glacier on the west side of the peak and ends up on the southwest ridge. All the major peaks in the Rize Kackar appear to have at least one easy route, usually up the south side. However, there is much scope for rock climbing, with face climbs of more than 1000 feet on good rock. There are a number of pinnacles which offer no easy way up. The Black Sea coast in this region is very wet and the northern slopes of the mountains are covered by luxuriant forest up to about 6000 feet.

The highest mountain in central Turkey is 12,848-foot Erciyas Dagi, a volcano 15 miles south of Kayseri. It is a one-day climb from Tekir Yaylasi on the east slope at 7000 feet; a ski lift can be used for the first part of the ascent above Tekir Yaylasi. The climb is easy until the final 65-foot summit pinnacle, which requires rope. There is a small glacier on the north side of the mountain.

The Aladag Mountains, some 50 miles north of Adana, are the highest part of the Tauras Range. These are steep rock peaks, many of which, including the highest, 12,251-foot Demirkazik, offer no nonroped route. Demirkazik is a two-day climb from Cukurbag, which is reached by road from Nigde.

The closest big mountain to Istanbul is 8343-foot Ulu Dag (also known as Mt. Olympus), 70 miles south of the city. It is known primarily for its skiing, and its ascent is an easy hike in summer.

▲ IRAN ▲

Elburz Mountains

Mt. Demavend: The highest mountain in Iran is the 18,603-foot volcano Mt. Demavend, about which Iranians feel the same way the Japanese do about Mt. Fuji. Like Fuji, the symmetrical cone of Demavend is a part of the daily scene for millions of people, including nomads far into the interior of the country, sailors 100 miles from shore on the Caspian Sea, and residents of cosmopolitan Tehran, which is just 50 miles southwest of the peak.

The climbing base for Mt. Demavend is the small town of Reineh, on the southeast slope of the mountain at about 7000 feet. Reineh is 60 miles by road from Tehran. Guides and mules are available here, and there is a hut operated by the Iranian Mountaineering Federation (main office address: Varzesh Avenue, Tehran). From Reineh the summit climb is usually made in two days, the first of which is spent packing in to a shelter high on the south slope. There are no technical difficulties on this route up Demavend, but there is a confusing welter of trails on the lower slopes, so the use of a guide is recommended.

The upper slopes of Demavend are characterized by loose scree, but much of it can be avoided by following the gullies that radiate downward from the summit. These gullies are snow filled until late summer. In early summer they provide long glissades with an altitude drop of as much as 7000 feet, provided climbers make the descent before the midday sun softens the snow. The only glacier on the peak is on the northern slope. During the summer there is little precipitation on Demavend, but there is occasional mist. The "climbing season" is considered to be from early summer to early fall.

The sulphur fumes which emanate from vents near the top of Demavend are sometimes quite strong, and have been known to deliver the *coup de grâce* to the summit hopes of climbers who were already a bit queasy from the rarefied air. The crater itself is filled with ice. After struggling up the southern slope of the peak, the climber reaching the summit sees a remarkable panorama to the north. Only 45 miles away are the subtropical marshes along the shore of the Caspian Sea, which is 90 feet below sea level. Unlike the barren slopes one passes on the approach from Tehran, the Caspian side of the Elburz Mountains is forested up to about 8000 feet.

Mt. Towchal: As a conditioner for Demavend, 12,977-foot Mt. Towchal is an easy climb which can be made in one day from Tehran.

Alam Kuh: The most alpine portion of the Elburz Mountains is the Takht-e Soleyman group which claims Iran's second highest mountain, 15,817-foot Alam Kuh. Alam Kuh has a 2000-foot-high wall which is perhaps the greatest rock-climbing challenge in Iran. The normal route up the peak is a nontechnical rock scramble. From the village of Rood-barak (4100 feet), which is northeast of Alam Kuh, there is a one-day pack-in to the Sarchal climber's hut at about

12,000 feet; from there the summit can be reached in a day. Roodbarak is a 115-mile drive from Tehran. There are several small glaciers in the Takht-e Soleyman group.

Kuh-e Sabalan: Iran's third highest peak is Kuh-e Sabalan, a 15,784-foot volcano 85 miles east of Tabriz.

Zagros Mountains

The Zagros Mountains parallel the western edge of Iran all the way from Azerbaijan to south of the city of Shiraz. They are fold mountains which consist largely of parallel ridges along a northwest-to-southeast axis. There is a large variety of forms, with some of the summits being rounded and elongated, while others are sharp and jagged. The range is characterized by deep gorges, particularly where rivers cut across the high parallel ridges. Between the ridges there are a few relatively level valleys which are cultivated, but most of the inhabitants of the region are nomadic. At one time there were some forests, particularly on the moister western slope, but few trees remain today. Almost all the yearly precipitation falls in the winter as snow, which lasts until late spring on the higher mountains; with the melting of the snow, meadows appear and the nomads move up to the higher slopes.

The highest of the several peaks in the range which exceed 14,000 feet is Zard Kuh (14,921 feet), 95 miles west of Isfahan. It can be climbed in about five hours from the Kouhrang Dam, which is reached by road from Isfahan. There are no technical difficulties, but climbers should hire a local guide to show the way.

Southern Iran

Among the barren volcanoes that dot southern Iran from the end of the Zagros to the Pakistan border, there are some that rise 7000 or 8000 feet above the desert. The highest are Kuh-e Hazarah (14,500 feet) and Kuh-e Laleh Zar (14,350 feet), both about 60 miles south of Kerman. Sixty-five miles south-southeast of Zahedan and less than 30 miles from the Pakistan border is the massive, still-active volcano Kuh-e Taftan (13,262 feet).

▲ CEYLON & SOUTHERN INDIA ▲

The verdant mountains of Ceylon are not high, but for hikers and students of comparative religion, if not for alpinists, they are by no means lacking in interest. The highest peak, 8281-foot Pidurutalagala, can be climbed by a good trail in about three hours from the mountain resort of Nuwara Eliya (6250 feet). The best-known and most interesting mountain on the island, however, is the sacred Adam's Peak (7360 feet), which has been climbed by hundreds of thousands of pilgrims over the last thouand years or more. The reverence in which the peak is held results from an indentation in the summit rocks which resembles an oversized footprint. As the name of the peak suggests, one legend has it that the print was made by Adam himself, but other tales attribute it to

Siva, St. Thomas, or Buddha. Pilgrims usually climb the peak at night in order to avoid the heat, and to see the sunrise from the top. The 3306 stone steps that lead to the summit are well lit, and iron railings provide security on the upper portion, where the rocky summit pyramid juts above the jungle.

One can also find pleasant hiking in the cool highlands of southern India, notably in the Nilgiri Hills and the Anamalai Hills. Dodabetta (8647 feet), the highest summit in the Nilgiris, is easily accessible from the mountain-resort town of Ootacamund (7000 feet). The less-visited Anamalai Hills, halfway between the Nilgiris and Cape Comorin, claim the highest point in southern India, 8841-foot Anaimudi. The Nilgiri and Anamalai regions are both essentially grassy tablelands, and the highest elevations are hills which rise 1000 feet or so above the general level.

▲ CENTRAL ASIA ▲

The greatest mountains on earth are those of Central Asia. The Hindu Kush, the Pamirs, the Tien Shan, the Kun Lun, the Amne Machin, the Karakoram, the Ta Hsueh Shan, the Himalayas, and several lesser ranges that rise above the Tibetan plateau all have mountains higher than the highest anywhere else on earth. Needless to say, in none of these ranges are the highest summits accessible to the casual, non-expeditionary climber for whom this book is primarily intended. However, in order to make the handbook complete, a brief description of the major ranges of Central Asia is included here.

A.   *The Himalayas:* The Himalayas are bounded on the west by the great bend of the Indus, and on the east by the great bend of the Brahmaputra; they are a 1500-mile-long arc separating the Tibetan plateau from the Indian subcontinent. Of the 14 peaks in the world over 8000 meters (26,248 feet), 10 are in the Himalayas.

The fascinating city of Kathmandu, Nepal is the base for two kinds of mountain adventure: climbing and trekking. The climbing, at least on the highest peaks, is usually undertaken by officially sponsored expeditions, though there are also many superb mountains within the reach of small private parties. (However, since 1965 no expeditions, official or private, have been permitted to the major peaks; the Nepalese government has not allowed foreign climbers to climb near the Tibetan border in order to avoid irritating the Chinese government. Expeditions to some peaks, including Everest, are to be permitted again beginning in 1969, but many others are still on the prohibited list. Information on the current status of the restrictions can be obtained from one's diplomatic representative in Nepal.)

Trekking has much to recommend it. For one thing, it allows the mountain lover who is not qualified for, or not interested in, expeditionary climbing to travel in the Himalayas. For another, it is easy to arrange, both logistically and politically. In fact, all-inclusive trekking tours are of-

MAP 37.   ROUTE TO EVEREST BASE CAMP

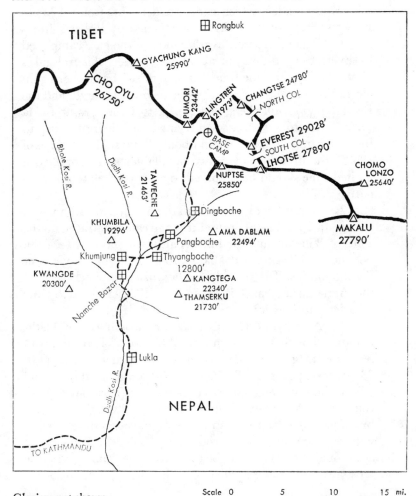

Glaciers not shown

Scale 0   5   10   15 mi.

ferred by an organization called Mountain Travel (P. O. Box 170, Kathmandu), which is operated by Lt. Colonel James Roberts. Some of the treks recommended by Roberts are:

1. Round trip from Kathmandu to the base camp used by Everest expeditions, at about 18,000 feet; this trek takes about 35 days, but the time can be reduced by chartering an aircraft to one of three airstrips between Kathmandu and the Everest region. Of these, the closest to Everest is at Lukla (9200 feet), from where, by hurrying a bit, the round trip to the base camp can be made in about 10 days. However, as of 1968, aircraft were not always available, and people with limited time should be prepared to accept a trek to an alternative destination.

2. A trek from Pokhara into the Annapurna-Dhaulagiri region. In 20 or 25 days round trip one can penetrate into the zone of Tibetan and Buddhist culture in northern Nepal, but shorter hikes from Pokhara also provide superb views of the mountains. The roughly 30-day hike completely around the Annapurna massif is not at present permitted by the Nepalese authorities.

3. A trek into the high country just north of Kathmandu: though there aren't any "8000-ers" here, one can see some magnificent mountains on the order of 22,000 to 23,000 feet; possible treks include: (a) about 15 days round trip to the Langtang Valley (11,500 feet); (b) about 10 days round trip to the Gosiankund Lakes (14,000 feet), returning by way of the Helmu district, with its interesting Sherpa villages; this trek involves crossing a pass over 15,000 feet; an additional five days should be planned if one wants to visit the most attractive Sherpa villages in Helmu; (c) a 20 to 25-day

trek which includes Helmu, the Gosiankund Lakes, and the Langtang Valley.

4. A 10-day trek from Kathmandu to Pokhara, offering fine views of the mountains.

For trekking in the lowlands below 7000 or 8000 feet (for instance, between Kathmandu and Pokhara) the best season is the winter. For high-country trekking, spring or fall are better, because it gets very cold in winter above 12,000 or 13,000 feet. The monsoon months, usually early June to late September, are suitable for neither hiking nor climbing in Nepal.

For climbers interested in exploration and first ascents in the Himalayas and Karakoram, an article by Dennis Gray in the September 1968 issue of *Summit* magazine gives a good outline of the first ascent possibilities that remain. As of that date the highest unclimbed summit was Gasherbrum III (26,088 feet) in the Karakoram. Other major peaks which will demand the utmost from climbers include Khinyang Chish (25,762 feet) in the Karakoram, and the Himalayan giants Menlungste (23,560 feet) and Gaurisankar (23,440 feet), both of which are northeast of Kathmandu.

Casual climbers and hikers who want to combine a trek with the thrill of standing on a "Himalayan summit" can find peaks on the order of 18,000 feet which are not technically difficult and which can be climbed with only a trekking permit; one might even be able to find an unclimbed peak or two in this category, particularly in western Nepal. On the southern slope of the Himalayas, the snowline varies from about 14,000 feet in the east, which receives the full brunt of the monsoon, to about 16,500 feet in the west.

B. *Karakoram:* On the map the Karakoram look like little more than an appendage of the Himalayas, but the range contains a concentration of mountain magnificence perhaps not equaled in any area of like size in the Himalayas themselves. The four 8000-meter peaks outside the Himalayas are all in the Karakoram. The 28,253-foot K2, second highest peak on earth, is a steep pyramid which in form, if not in height, outshines Everest.

C. *The Kun Lun system:* The Kun Lun, including its eastern extensions, is the longest mountain system in Asia. The range begins near the western tip of Sinkiang and consists of one main crest until about 82° east longitude, where it splits into two ranges, the Astin Tagh on the north, and the Arka Tagh on the south; the Tibet-Sinkiang border follows the latter. Outside of the Himalaya-Karakoram system, it is probable that the two highest mountains on earth are in the Arka Tagh: Ulugh Muztagh (25,340 feet) and Bokalikh Tagh (25,329 feet). It is doubtful if either had been climbed as of 1968. The snowline in the western part of the Kun Lun is about 14,500 feet, but farther east the extreme dryness causes it to rise to nearly 20,000 feet, the highest in the world with the possible exception of the Puna de Atacama region in Chile and Argentina.

During World War II, reports drifted out of China of a group of mountains in central Chinghai which might top Mt. Everest. The reports were soon proven wrong, but their very existence at such a late date emphasized the remoteness of the mountains in question, the Chishih (or Amne Machin) Range, which are an eastern branch of the Kun Lun. The

Chinese climbed 23,490-foot Amne Machin Peak in 1960.

D. *Ta Hsueh Shan:* Of the mountains of truly Himalayan proportions, the most easterly are the Ta Hsueh Shan, which reach 24,900 feet in Minya Konka; this great snow pyramid is just 150 miles southwest of Chengtu, the capital of China's Szechuan Province. Minya Konka was first climbed in 1932 by two young Americans, Richard Burdsall and Terris Moore, in a remarkable demonstration of what a small do-it-yourself expedition can achieve; it was the highest summit attained by American climbers until the ascent of 26,470-foot Hidden Peak in 1958.

E. *Pamirs:* The Pamirs occupy the wild area where the Soviet Union, China, and Afghanistan meet. The greater portion of the range is in the Tadzhik S. S. R., but the highest peaks, Kungur Tagh (25,325 feet), Kungur Tjube Tagh (24,919 feet), and Muztagh Ata (24,758 feet) are across the border in China's Sinkiang Province; the two last-named peaks were first climbed in 1956 by joint Russo-Chinese parties, but Kungur Tagh was apparently unclimbed as of 1968. On the Muztagh Ata climb there were 19 Russians and 12 Chinese, which must be something of a record number of climbers for a major first-ascent party. The highest peak in the Soviet portion of the Pamirs, and in the entire Soviet Union, is 24,590-foot Pik Communism, which was first climbed in 1933 by a Soviet party.

F. *Tien Shan:* The Tien Shan extend northeastward from the Pamirs, forming the Sino-Soviet border for some 400 miles; then the boundary turns north while the range continues eastward into the center of China's Sinkiang Province. The highest mountain in the Tien Shan and the second highest in the Soviet Union, Pik Pobeda (24,406 feet), was first climbed in 1938 by a Soviet party.

G. *Hindu Kush:* The Hindu Kush extend from the Pamirs into central Afghanistan, decreasing steadily in height toward the west. The highest summit, 25,230-foot Tirich Mir, was climbed in 1950 by a Norwegian expedition. The most westerly extension of the Hindu Kush is the Koh-i-Baba Range, the highest point of which is 16,874 feet.

The World's Highest Mountains

Here is a list of the 14 peaks in the world over 8000 meters (26,248 feet) in height—all in the Himalayas (H) or the Karakoram (K)—giving the dates of the first ascents and the nationalities of the climbers:

Order, Name	Height in feet (and meters)	Date of first ascent	Nationalities of first ascent parties
1. Mt. Everest (H)	29,028 (8848)	1953	British (actually a New Zealander and a Sherpa reached the summit)
2. K2 (K)	28,253 (8611)	1954	Italian
3. Kanchenjunga (H)	28,168 (8585)	1955	British
4. Lhotse (H)	27,890 (8501)	1956	Swiss
5. Makalu (H)	27,790 (8470)	1955	French
6. Dhaulagiri (H)	26,811 (8172)	1960	Swiss/Austrian
7. Cho Oyu (H)	26,750 (8153)	1954	Austrian (and two Sherpas)

8. Manaslu (H)	26,658 (8125)	1956	Japanese (and a Sherpa)
9. Nanga Parbat (H)	26,658 (8125)	1953	German expedition (the Austrian Hermann Buhl reached the summit alone)
10. Annapurna (H)	26,504 (8078)	1950	French
11. Hidden Peak (or Gasherbrum I) (K)	26,470 (8068)	1958	American
12. Broad Peak (K)	26,400 (8047)	1957	Austrian
13. Gasherbrum II (K)	26,360 (8035)	1956	Austrian
14. Gosianthan (or Shisha Pangma) (H)	26,291 (8013)	1964 (?)	Chinese claim first ascent

(Note: For a list of the 61 peaks over 7500 meters [24,607 feet] see *The American Alpine Journal* for 1964.)

▲ ALTAI MOUNTAINS ▲

The Altai Mountains are shared by the Soviet Union, Mongolia, and China. The greater portion of the 1200-mile-long chain is in Mongolia, but the most alpine section is in the Soviet Union, which claims the highest summit, 14,783-foot Gora Belukha in the Katun Range. The highest mountain in the Mongolian Altai is 14,311-foot Monho Hayrhan Uula, which is second only to Gora Belukha in height. The third highest Altai summit is the heavily glaciated 14,291-foot Kuitun in the Taban Bogdo Uula massif at the junction of the three countries.

The Soviet Altai is a complex system of high ridges separated from each other by broad valleys, some of which are quite flat and covered by steppe vegetation. One such steppe lies at the northern foot of the Katun Range at about 3300 feet elevation. The snowline in the Soviet Altai varies from about 7600 feet in the northwest to 10,200 feet in the southeast; in Mongolia it rises progressively higher toward the southeast. The glaciers in the range total approximately 230 square miles. Timberline varies from 6300 feet to 8000 feet, northwest to southeast. The intermountain valleys are settled up to an elevation of well over 5000 feet.

Gora Belukha is a twin-peaked mountain which is covered by glaciers (totaling about 27 square miles of ice) except for some sharp ridges and rocky outcroppings. The higher eastern peak and the western peak (14,563 feet) are joined by a snow-covered saddle which slopes gently to the south but falls steeply to the north.

▲ SIBERIA ▲

Siberia is as big as the entire United States with a couple of extra Alaskas thrown in for good measure. Most of this vast area is lowland forest or steppe, but there are some impressive mountains in eastern and southern Siberia. The highest mountain in Siberia and the highest active volcano in the Eastern Hemisphere is 15,584-foot Klyuchevskaya on the Kamchatka peninsula. Klyuchevskaya is a near-perfect Fuji-like cone whose regular contours are maintained by frequent eruptions of volcanic ash. Another factor in preserving the cone's symmetry is that to a considerable depth the slopes are frozen solid, thereby retarding erosion. The snowline on the mountain is about 5300 feet, but some glacial tongues descend to below 4000 feet. Kamchatka is one of the most active volcanic regions on earth; altogether there are some 127 volcanoes, of which about 13 are still active. There are several other volcanoes over 11,000 feet, but no others exceed 12,000 feet.

In northeastern Siberia (aside from Kamchatka) there are many important mountain ranges of which the Chersky Mountains are the highest. The highest peak in the range, Gora Pobeda (10,325 feet), rises over 7000 feet above timberline and has some glaciers; however, because of the low precipitation the range has fewer glaciers than one might expect for such northern latitudes. The total area of ice in the northeastern Siberian ranges is perhaps half that of the Altais. Much of the Chersky Range, as well as other nearby ranges, consists of bald, rounded mountains, but there are a few areas with steeper, more alpine relief. The Suntar Khayata Range, southwest of the Chersky Range, is perhaps the most alpine in northeastern Siberia; here one finds sharp, jagged crests and the most extensive glaciers in the region. The Suntar Khayata reach 9708 feet in Gora Mus Khaya.

East of the Altai Mountains there is an almost unbroken series of mountain ranges all the way to the Sea of Okhotsk, a distance of 2000 miles. Just east of the Altais is the Tannu Ola Range, the highest and most rugged portion of which is in the west, near where it joins the Altais. Here Munku Khayrhan-Ula reaches 12,982 feet and carries a few small glaciers. North of the Tannu Ola are the Western Sayan Mountains, which reach 9613 feet in Gora Karamosh. Most of this range has rounded summits, but there are also several areas with jagged rock peaks, especially the Yergak and Aradanskiy groups. The Eastern Sayans extend to Lake Baikal, and reach 11,453 feet in Gora Munku Sardyk. The top 2000 feet on this peak has two small glaciers totaling less than half a square mile in area. Most of the Eastern Sayan has rounded summits but in several areas, including the Kryzhina and Agul Belki ranges, there are some more alpine mountains. In both the eastern and western Sayan there are large expanses of bald mountains above the timberline (which averages about 6400 feet). Anyone interested in tramping about southern Siberia could undoubtedly find good hiking and backpacking in these mountains.

East of Lake Baikal are the Stanovoy Mountains, where the highest peak, 8094-foot Mt. Skalisty, rises about 3000 feet above timberline. The Stanovoy Mountains also have some sharp, craggy summits, but for the most part they are rounded and massive.

The western boundary of Siberia is the Ural Mountains, a long (1200 miles), narrow chain of mostly forest-covered hills, above which there rise a few rocky summits. In the north, where the highest peak, 6214-foot Gora Narodnaya, is found, there are some glaciers.

▲ NEW ZEALAND ▲

The Southern Alps of New Zealand rank among the world's great mountain ranges in everything but altitude, and at least for snow and ice climbers their challenge is no less than that of the European Alps. On the whole, fewer of the high peaks in the Southern Alps offer an easy "tourist route" than is the case with the European Alps. Mt. Cook, the highest peak in the Southern Alps, is only 12,349 feet above sea level, but it rises a full 8000 feet above the glaciers at its base. There is no easy route up Cook, and the local guides will not take inexperienced climbers to the summit.

Mt. Cook National Park encompasses the most important part of the Southern Alps. The administrative and tourist center of the park is the Hermitage, where there is a large hotel. Nearby is the Park Board Headquarters, where one can obtain climbing information and arrange to hire a guide; information can be obtained in advance by writing the Chief Ranger, Mt. Cook National Park. The Hermitage is 10 miles south of Mt. Cook, at 2500 feet elevation.

One can go by bus from the Hermitage to Ball Hut, which is southeast of Mt. Cook at 3600 feet. From here it is a half-day climb to the Plateau Hut (8000 feet), the most frequent starting point for climbing Cook. Above the Plateau Hut the route is via the Linda Glacier on the northeast side of the mountain. Though this is the easiest route, it is considered dangerous because of the frequent avalanches. A number of other routes up Cook have been climbed, including all the faces except the southeast (Caroline), which is continuously raked by avalanches.

The first ascent of Mt. Cook, in 1894, concluded a tense international race. In 1882 the Rev. W. S. Green, an Englishman, and two Swiss guides had made the first serious attempt and had come within a few hundred feet of succeeding in reaching the summit.

They were followed by several more unsuccessful attempts, after each of which the competition became fiercer. In late 1894, New Zealand climbers learned that the well-known English climber E. A. Fitzgerald and the Swiss guide Mattias Zurbriggen—one of the best of the day—had set sail for New Zealand bent on scaling Cook. When the local climbers learned of this threat to their national pride they went all out, and on Christmas Eve Tom Fyfe, George Graham, and Jack Clarke reached the summit. Fitzgerald was so disheartened

MAP 38. MT. COOK REGION, New Zealand

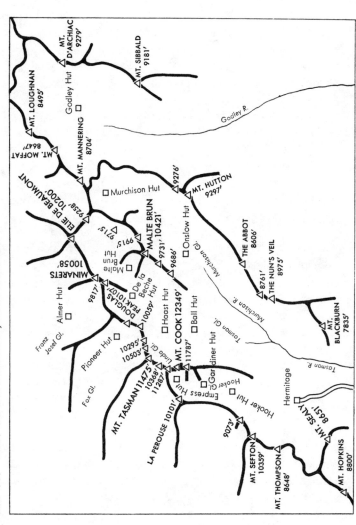

Scale 0 1 2 3 4 5 6 mi.

Glaciers not shown (though a few major ones named)

that he made no attempt on Cook, though he did make a number of other first ascents in the range.

Climbers with limited experience who want to climb in the Southern Alps should direct their attention to peaks other than Mt. Cook or the second highest peak in the range, 11,475-foot Mt. Tasman, which is also a difficult ice climb. Of the 17 peaks over 10,000 feet in Mt. Cook National Park, the Minarets (10,058), Elie de Beaumont (10,200), and Malte Brun (10,421) are perhaps the least difficult, and the Minarets can be climbed on skis. Compared to the European Alps, the Southern Alps offer relatively little rock climbing, though some can be found on a number of routes, including the north and south ridges of Mt. Cook. In general the rock, which is sandstone, is loose and shattered. The favorite peak of rock climbers in Mt. Cook National Park is Malte Brun. For hikers and less ambitious climbers, the Park has several peaks of 7000 or 8000 feet which involve nothing more than scrambling; one of the higher of these is 8651-foot Mt. Sealy.

The Southern Alps and the European Alps are about the same distance from the Equator, but the permanent snowline of the former—approximately 7000 feet in the Cook region —averages 2000 feet lower than that of the latter. Furthermore, the greater accumulation of snow causes the New Zealand glaciers to flow faster and to reach farther below the snowline. For instance, the Fox Glacier on the wet western slope of the Southern Alps reaches down to below 700 feet elevation. Skiers will find runs over 15 miles long on the glaciers of Mt. Cook National Park. Specially equipped ski-planes are used instead of tows.

The Southern Alps extend for some 450 miles—almost the full length of South Island—and only a small section is included in Mt. Cook National Park. Near the southern tip of the island is Fjordland National Park where the famous spearlike monolith Mitre Peak rises a precipitous mile right out of the water. When viewed from the hotel at Milford Sound the peak looks virtually unscalable, but there is a non-technical route up the back side (via the east ridge). In Fjordland rock climbers will find the firm granite missing in the Cook region, but they must be prepared for almost daily cold rain. The southern part of the range also contains some fine alpine mountains, though they are lower than those of the Cook region. Among the many noteworthy peaks are Mt. Aspiring (9959 feet), which has been called the "Matterhorn of New Zealand," and 9042-foot Mt. Tutoko, the "Monarch of Fjordland." Tutoko has an extraordinary 6000-foot-high unclimbed south face which is swept by avalanches many times a day. Apart from the Mt. Cook area and parts of Fjordland, access to the high peaks of the Southern Alps is poor and often involves long treks of several days up trailless valleys. In many of the access valleys rivers are unbridged and the fording of mountain torrents is common and can be hazardous.

The major mountains of New Zealand's North Island are volcanoes. The highest is 9175-foot Ruapehu, one of several volcanoes in Tongariro National Park near the center of the island. Ruapehu has a few small glaciers near the summit, but can be climbed quite easily; crampons and ice axes might be useful, depending on the season. The crater contains a lake of warm water at 8500 feet, and climbers might well take along swimming suits for a delightful—albeit sulphurous—dip in this unique naturally heated mountaintop swimming pool. One of New Zealand's best-developed ski areas is on Ruapehu's western slope. A ski tow which begins at the Ruapehu Alpine Village (5300 feet) reaches to within about an hour's hike of the crater lake.

Near the southwest tip of North Island is the well-preserved cone of Mt. Egmont (8260 feet), which can be climbed from the north, south, or east. Paved roads reach about 3000 feet elevation on all three sides. The climb is not technically difficult but the mountain has taken its toll of novices through exposure.

New Zealand's summer is of course America's winter. The climbing season is roughly November through April in the Southern Alps; some of the rock peaks such as Malte Brun can be climbed for several weeks after the ice peaks like Mt. Cook have been closed because of avalanche danger.

▲ AUSTRALIA ▲

Australia is the least mountainous of the continents and the only one on which there are no peaks high enough to carry glaciers. The highest summit is 7316-foot Mt. Kosciusko in the Snowy Mountains, 200 miles east-northeast of Melbourne. There used to be a motorable road up Kosciusko from Charlotte Pass, but it has been closed to vehicles in order to preserve wilderness values; the summit is now accessible only to skiers in winter and hikers in summer. Kosciusko and a few other peaks are high enough to climb above the treeline.

The most unusual mountain scenery in Australia is near the center of the continent, where strangely shaped sandstone hogbacks and monoliths rise above the desert. Ayers Rock (2845 feet), 200 miles southwest of Alice Springs, is a reddish dome that leaps 1100 feet right out of a perfectly flat plain. It is an easy climb with the help of a railing installed to aid tourists. Mt. Olga (3507 feet) is an improbable looking group of 1500-foot-high rounded knobs a few miles west of Ayers Rock.

Australia's most alpine peaks are not actually on the continent at all, but on the island of Tasmania. Though low, the mountains of Tasmania are surprisingly spectacular and rock climbers can find peaks which do not offer any non-roped routes. The highest on the island is Mt. Ossa (5305 feet), which is a four- or five-mile hike from the Petion Hut; some scrambling is involved near the top.

▲ PHILIPPINES ▲

For anyone with a bent for exploration the Philippines have much to offer, though the greatest attraction is undoubtedly seaward rather than hillward. Among the 7000-plus islands that make up the country, many are uninhabited and virtually unexplored, while some are inhabited by aboriginal tribes which have had almost no contact with modern Philippine culture. Nevertheless, although the most important piece of equipment for exploring the islands is a boat, it is also possible to get plenty of good use out of a pair of hiking boots.

The highest mountain in the Philippines is Mt. Apo (9690 feet), 25 miles southwest of Davao on Mindanao Island. From Barrio Sibulan, which is southeast of the peak at 2000 feet elevation, the round trip to the top of Mt. Apo can be made in about three days. There is a trail to the summit region, and guides and porters are available locally.

The best-known and most impressive mountain in the Philippines is Mayon Volcano (8284 feet), near the port of Legaspi at the southeastern tip of Luzon. Rising in one sweep directly from the sea to its full height, this is truly a major mountain; and it is generally considered to be the most perfect volcanic cone on earth. The steep eight-mile trail to its summit begins at Barrio Buyuan, on the southeast flank at 1000 feet. The trail is not easy to follow, and one should hire a local guide. The climb is usually done in two days round trip. Mayon has erupted at least seven times in this century, most recently in 1968. For a time after each eruption, the unsettled volcanic ash on the higher slopes makes for very difficult, if not impossible, footing.

The highest summit on Luzon is 9612-foot Pulog, 25 miles northeast of the mountain-resort town of Baguio.

▲ NEW GUINEA ▲

West Irian

There are few mountains which are less known or more interesting than those of western New Guinea, or West Irian as it is now called. Here, just 4° south of the Equator, the Snow Mountains thrust above the jungle to a height of about 16,500 feet (5030 meters) in twin-summitted Sukarno Peak (formerly called Ngapalu), which is only slightly higher than several other peaks on a long limestone ridge extending from northwest to southeast. On the northeast side of this ridge there is a huge escarpment up to 3000 feet high and many miles in length. In sharp contrast to the escarpment, the southwest side of the ridgeline is a gentle, glacier-covered slope. The glaciers stretch almost unbroken across the entire breadth of the slope, a distance of several miles, and extend down to about 14,500 feet. The glaciers drain into the Merendal Basin, a U-shaped valley which opens to the west. Sukarno Peak is near the eastern, closed, end of the "U." About two miles south-southeast of Sukarno Peak is another mountain nearly as high, East Carstenz Top (*ca.* 16,437 feet, or 5010 meters; there may be a new name for this peak). Another ridge, the other arm of the "U," extends westward from East Carstenz Top. This ridge contains Yayakusumu,

MAP 39. SUKARNO PEAK, New Guinea

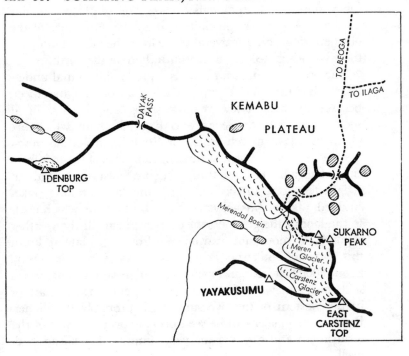

Scale 0   1   2   3   4 mi.

which is apparently slightly lower than Sukarno Peak, though some sources state that it is higher. The south face of this southern ridge is less precipitous than the north face of the northern ridge, but the overall slope from the mountaintops to the lowlands is steeper on the south than on the north.

The ascent of Sukarno Peak is a pretty substantial undertaking, but the time required is less than one might expect, because in the last few years airstrips have been built at such settlements as Beoga and Ilaga, both of which are about five days' march (*ca.* 35 or 40 airline miles) northeast of the mountains. The first three or four days of the trek from either Beoga or Ilaga are through dense forest; then, at about 10,500 feet, one breaks out onto the large, rolling, lake-studded, mainly grass-covered Kemabu Plateau, which leads to the foot of the great northeast escarpment. If the weather is good, the mountains can be seen from this plateau. From this direction Sukarno Peak appears as twin rock towers about 3000 feet high and joined by a high saddle. The towers stick out somewhat from the escarpment but are part of it; the western of the two summits is probably the higher. Parts of the glacier can be seen peeking over the crest of the escarpment and capping the very summit of Sukarno Peak itself.

There is of course no "standard route" up Sukarno Peak, but in 1964 a Japanese-Indonesian party led by Taian Kato found what may be as easy a route as any, as indicated by the fact that it was the first mountain climb for the three Indonesians who reached the top. The party ascended a gully some distance to the west of the peak to reach the crestline, and then crossed the glacier to the summit. A steep ice fall requiring step-cutting was the main technical problem encountered on the glacier.

The peak now known as Sukarno Peak appears to have first been climbed by a Dutch party led by Dr. A. H. Colijn in 1936. Heinrich Harrer also ascended this peak, plus many others in the range, and made the first ascent of Yayakusumu, in 1962. Yayakusumu had repulsed a concerted attack by the Colijn party in 1936, and it turned out to require fairly difficult rock climbing. This peak is certainly the most technically demanding of the major peaks in the range.

There has been considerable confusion about the identities of the highest summits in the Snow Mountains. Before Indonesia acquired West Irian, the highest peak was known as Carstenz Top or Mt. Carstenz. The latter term could have been used to denote the whole ridge, but just which peak the hypothetical Carstenz Top was supposed to be is unclear, because no one was really sure which peak was the highest. Assuming that sources indicating that the highest summit is 16,500-foot Sukarno Peak are correct, then the peak that Colijn knew as Ngapalu (i.e., Sukarno Peak) would actually have been Carstenz Top.

A few miles west of the high ridge containing Sukarno Peak is the Idenburg Range which reaches about 15,748 feet (4800 meters) in Idenburg Peak. This peak, which carries a small icecap, was first climbed by Harrer's party, which found it easy. About 100 miles east of Sukarno Peak, the Snow Mountains again reach above the snowline in Trikora (formerly Wilhelmina) Peak (*ca.* 15,585 feet), which was first climbed by a Dutch party in 1912.

The climate in the Snow Mountains is comparable to that of the glaciated ranges of the Ruwenzori in Africa and the Sierra Nevada de Cocuy in Colombia, which also rise directly above steaming equatorial jungles. Colijn's, Harrer's, and Kato's parties all climbed between December and March, and found that at that time of year there were at least a few clear moments on most days, although there was much rain and mist.

Australian New Guinea

Climbing the major peaks of Indonesian New Guinea still requires quite a substantial expedition, but the ascent of the highest mountain in Australian New Guinea, Mt. Wilhelm (earlier maps gave 15,400 feet, but more recent ones show 14,786 feet), is a much simpler matter requiring only two days of actual hiking. The starting point for climbing Mt. Wilhelm is the airstrip at Keglsugl, which is located about six miles southeast of the summit at 8350 feet elevation. One can reach Keglsugl by air or road. Guides and porters are available at Keglsugl by pre-arrangement.

There is an old native trail which takes about four hours from Keglsugl to Lake Aunde (11,700 feet), near timberline, where there is a small hut. For the first mile above Keglsugl there are some native farms, but then one enters a dense moss-covered rain forest which lasts all the way to timberline. From Lake Aunde the trail continues up steep, grassy slopes to the summit ridge which requires some easy scrambling. Mt. Wilhelm is the culminating point of a series of rugged ridges; it is rivaled in height and interest by other nearby peaks, of which Mt. Herbert, a steep rock pyramid to the west, looks the most challenging. From the summit of Mt. Wilhelm on a clear day the ocean is visible 50 miles to the north.

The annual rainfall in the Wilhelm region is about 175 inches. The wettest months are January through March. The driest period is May through September, though even then it rains about one day in two. Clouds usually form by 9:00 A.M., so an early start from Lake Aunde is desirable. It sometimes snows during the night above 14,000 feet, but there is rarely any snow left after midmorning.

The highest summit of the Owen Stanley Range in southeastern New Guinea is Mt. Victoria (13,363 feet), some 50 miles northeast of the town of Port Moresby. Because of its relative visibility and accessibility from populated areas, Mt. Victoria was the first of New Guinea's high mountains to attract the attention of explorers. It was first climbed in 1889 by an expedition led by Sir William MacGregor.

▲ BORNEO ▲

A large portion of Borneo is hilly, but with one exception the hills are not high enough to rise above the jungle. That exception is Mt. Kinabalu (13,455 feet), a granitic massif 5000 feet higher than any other mountain on the island. This magnificent mountain near the northern tip of Borneo rises in one almost unbroken sweep only 25 miles from the South China Sea.

On the map Mt. Kinabalu is shaped like a "U," with the two arms aimed toward the north. The highest part of the mountain is the curve at the bottom of the "U," where there is a large rolling platform of smooth, barren rock, which covers more than a square mile at an altitude between 12,500 to 13,000 feet. From the summit platform rise many pinnacles and knobs, the highest of which is 13,455-foot Low's Peak—named after Hugh Low, the British colonial official who made the first ascent of the mountain in 1851. Low's Peak is a gentle knob which can be climbed in an easy scramble, but some of the pinnacles are nearly vertical on all sides, well over 200 feet high, and probably unclimbed. The summit platform crowns tremendous precipices which thrust above the rain forest that covers the lower slopes of the mountain. The upper limit of the forest is about 11,000 feet, above which the entire mountain is bare rock, except for some scrub-filled gullies. The smooth, bare surface is accounted for by the fact that the heavy rainfall washes soil off the mountain before it can accumulate. It rarely, if every, snows on Mt. Kinabalu, but it occasionally freezes on the summit during the night.

The greatest of the cliffs that surround the mountain are the west face of Alexandra Peak (13,132 feet) and the walls of Low's Gully. Alexandra's is the farthest west of the peaks which rise above the summit platform, and from its summit a sheer wall drops 3000 feet to the west. This wall would delight Yosemite climbers, but to reach its base would take days of

MAP 40.   MT. KINABALU, BORNEO

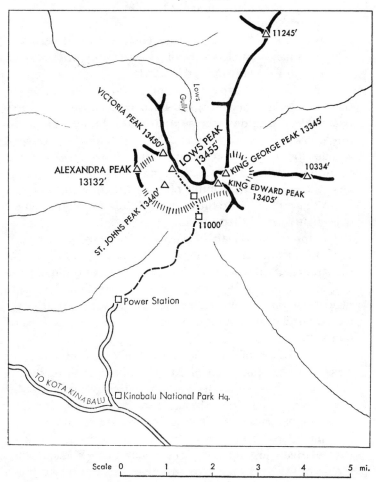

Scale 0   1   2   3   4   5 mi.

Outer Limit of Summit Plateau ||||||||||||

bushwhacking through almost impenetrable jungle. Low's Gully (a most inadequate name) is the stupendous 4000-foot deep chasm which lies between the two arms of the "U"; climbs of 4000 feet on good rock could be found here. Mt. Kinabalu has been climbed from Low's Gully at least once, by a party of Royal Marines in 1964.

The cliffs that surround the mountain are least steep on the south side, where a shrub-filled gully provides a non-technical passage onto the summit platform. At the base of this gully there is a climber's hut (11,000 feet) which is reached by trail from a power station (6000 feet) near the headquarters of Kinabalu National Park. At 12,500 feet, near the edge of the summit platform, there is another hut. From this higher hut to the summit of Low's Peak the route is over gently sloping bare rock.

The top of Mt. Kinabalu is usually in clouds by 9:00 A.M., so climbers who stay at the 11,000-foot hut should leave for the summit by dawn at the latest. Because of the danger of getting lost in the fog and being unable to find the shrub-filled gully on the descent, parties should hire a local guide, for whom arrangements can be made at the Park head-quarters.

The number of possible rock-climbing routes on the precipices and pinnacles of Mt. Kinabalu is virtually un-limited, but the mountain is not quite the climber's paradise it looks like. Aside from the fact that Borneo is a bit off the climber's beaten track, there is the problem of almost daily rain plus the fact that the only trail to the rock area is on the relatively unimpressive south side, which means that the great walls on the north and west sides are very difficult to reach. Nevertheless, one could spend weeks at the upper hut and enjoy fine climbing every day, including some first ascents of major pinnacles.

▲ INDONESIA ▲
(except West Irian)

All the islands of Indonesia are mountainous, and, outside of West Irian, most of the big mountains are volcanoes. The highest is 12,467-foot Kerentji, located about 80 miles southeast of Padang, on Sumatra. The trail up Kerentji begins at the village of Krisik Tuo, about 30 miles by motorable road from the town of Sungaipenuh, which is south-southeast of the mountain. From Krisik Tuo the climb is usually done in two days. The lower part of the trail is through cultivated country but one soon enters a zone of forest. There is a "rest house" (probably rather primitive) about eight hours up the trail. It takes about four hours from the rest house to the summit. Guides and porters should be available in Krisik Tuo or Kaju Aro, a tea estate that is passed on the road from Sungaipenuh.

Many of the volcanoes on Java are near villages which can be reached by motor vehicles, and are fairly frequently ascended. The highest on the island is Semeru (12,060 feet), located east of Malang in the eastern part of the island. Bali is topped by 10,308-foot Agung, which has erupted very destructively in recent years. The small and little-known island of Lombok, between Bali and Sumbawa, consists of little more than the great Rindjani (12,224 feet). Sumbawa is topped by 9353-foot Tamboro, whose eruption in 1815 was one of the greatest in modern times. (The island of Krakatoa, which disappeared in 1883 as a result of perhaps the greatest volcanic eruption in recorded history, has reappeared as a 2667-foot-high island between Sumatra and Java.) The most rugged and least known mountains in Indonesia (outside of West Irian) are on the chicken-foot-shaped island of Celebes, where the highest summit is probably about 11,500 feet.

▲ SOUTHEAST ASIA ▲

The highest elevations among the countries of Southeast Asia are along the Sino-Burmese border, where Hkakabo Razi reaches 19,295 feet. However, these mountains of northern Burma are actually just the outward extensions of the highlands of southwestern China. Outside of this frontier region, the highest mountain range in mainland Southeast Asia is the Naga Hills along the Indian-Burmese border.

Here the border peak Saramati (12,553 feet) is an imposing mountain which rises far above neighboring summits. Saramati's summit is about 1000 feet above timberline and wears a mantle of snow in winter.

The Arakan Range near the west coast of Burma is structurally a continuation of the Naga Hills. Mt. Victoria (10,015 feet), the highest summit, is covered by jungle right up to the top.

Burma is not the only mountainous country in Southeast Asia. The highest point in the forested mountains of northern Thailand is 8514-foot Doi Inthanon, 35 miles west-southwest of Chiang Mai. Laos is a country of mountains with an untold number of jungle-clad peaks and ridges over 6000 feet in elevation; the highest is probably 9246-foot Phou Bia, 30 miles south-southwest of Xieng Khouang. The hills of southern Cambodia reach 5948 feet in Mt. Aural, 60 miles northwest of Phnom Penh. The highest point in Malaya is 7186-foot Tahan in the cool Cameron Highlands about 100 miles north of Kuala Lumpur.

The best-known mountain range in Southeast Asia is the Annam Cordillera, which extends for about 400 miles from the vicinity of Xieng Khouang, in Laos, to the Central Highlands of South Vietnam; for most of this distance the range forms the border between Laos and Vietnam. The highest elevation, 8894 feet, is located on the border to the east of Xieng Khouang. In South Vietnam the highest peak is Ngoc Linh (8524 feet), 50 miles due north of Kontum.

The highest mountain in all Vietnam is in North Vietnam's Fan Si Pan Range, where Fan Si Pan Peak (10,308 feet) rises 20 miles south of the Yunnan border. But the most famous "mountains" in North Vietnam—and some of the most unusual on earth—are in Along Bay, just 25 miles east of Haiphong. Here perpendicular limestone peaks reminiscent of the Kueilin-Yangshuo region of China's Kwangsi Province rise out of the bay as islands.

It goes without saying that Southeast Asia offers little scope for mountaineering in the usual sense, but for travelers with a bent for exploration of rugged mountainous country populated by diverse ethnic groups, the region has much to offer. At present, unfortunately, with the exception of Thailand and Malaya, most of the highlands are off limits for political reasons to explorers on foot, but hopefully this situation will change before too many years have passed.

▲ TAIWAN ▲

Despite the fact that Taiwan leads the world in population density, the eastern half of the island is a virtually uninhabited wilderness of mountains, steep V-shaped valleys, and precipitous gorges. On the east coast, between the towns of Suao and Hualien, perpendicular cliffs rise hundreds of feet straight out of the water. Above the cliffs, the slopes ease off a bit but there are some quite high peaks very close to the water's edge. For instance, the 7897-foot summit of Chingshui Shan is only two-and-a-half miles inland. Remarkably, the only north-south road in eastern Taiwan has been carved out of the coastal cliffs, and in places this narrow one-lane

MAP 41. YU SHAN, TAIWAN

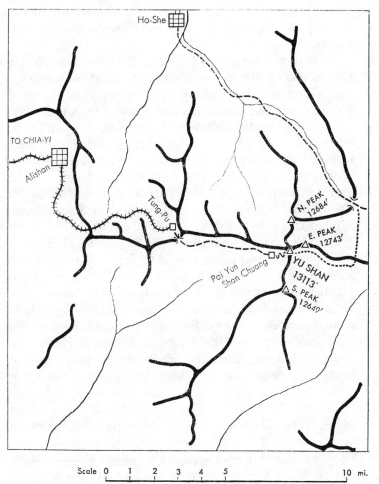

Ho-She

TO CHIA-YI

Alishan

Tung-Pu

N. PEAK
12684'

E. PEAK
12743'

Pai Yun
Shan Chuang

YU SHAN
13113'

S. PEAK
12649'

Scale 0   1   2   3   4   5   10 mi.

"East Coast Highway" is several hundred feet directly above the ocean. Near Hualien is Taiwan's best-known natural feature, Taroko Gorge, which is one of the greatest canyons in East Asia.

Taiwan's highest peak, 13,113-foot Yu Shan ("Jade Mountain"), also known as Mt. Morrison, rises above a series of high ridges and deep valleys near the center of the island. From the town of Chia-yi there is a tourist train to Alishan, a mountain resort at 7500 feet where guides can be hired for climbing Yu Shan; from Alishan an irregularly scheduled logging train runs about 12 miles to the small settlement of Tung-pu (9000 feet), where there is a small government-operated rest house, and where the trail to the summit begins. The trail leads in about five hours to Pai Yun Shan Chuang, a hut at 11,700 feet, which is some 300 feet below timberline. The trail continues from the hut to the summit, but it is in poor condition and hikers should be prepared to do a little scrambling. Yu Shan was first climbed in 1896 by a group of Japanese forestry officials led by Dr. Seiroku Honda.

Taiwan's second highest mountain, 12,743-foot Hsueh Shan (meaning "Snow Mountain") is a steep, three-day round-trip hike from the mountain village of Huan Shan (5600 feet), where guides are available. There is a trail up Hsueh Shan but in places it is very hard to find, so one should certainly hire a guide. The steepest peak on Taiwan is 11,722-foot Ta Pa Chien Shan, whose 400-foot-high summit tower of crumbling rock is nearly vertical on three sides and very steep on the fourth (west) side. Though ladders have been placed up the west face, they are poorly maintained and unreliable, so rope should be taken. Ta Pa Chien Shan is in a remote area north of Hsueh Shan, and a week should be allowed for the trip.

The best time for climbing in Taiwan is October and November, which is between the summer typhoons and the winter snows; April and May are next best. Additional information on climbing in Taiwan can be obtained from the Taiwan Mountaineering Association, 45 Tien Shui Rd., Taipei.

▲ EASTERN CHINA ▲

Traditional China, what Sinologists sometimes call "China Proper," consists of the relatively lowlands to the east of the great mountains and plateaus which cover the western half of China. The western edge of China Proper is roughly 105° east longitude, though the Tsinling Mountains, the easternmost extension of the Kun Lun Mountains, push beyond 112° into central Honan Province.

Though not high in elevation, this eastern half of China is by no means all level. In fact, the only extensive flatlands are the Yellow River and Manchurian plains. South of the Yangtze, one is almost never out of sight of mountains or hills. To many Chinese the most magnificent scenery in China—and therefore in the world—is the karst country of the Kueilin-Yangshuo region of Kwangsi Province (west of

Canton). Here is a unique landscape of sheer limestone peaks which rise as much as 1000 feet directly above the rice fields and villages at their bases. A good portion of China's landscape painting was inspired by this region. Other well-known massifs with sharp peaks worthy of the best traditional landscape painters are Huang Shan in Anhwei Province, and Hua Shan in Shensi Province.

In Chinese tradition there were five sacred mountains: Hengshan, in Shansi (the sacred mountain of the north); Tai Shan, in Shantung (east); Heng Shan, in Hunan (south); Hua Shan, in Shensi (west); and Sung Shan, in Honan (center). All of these have well-trod stone paths to their summits, and temples scattered about their slopes. So do hundreds of other less well-known mountains throughout eastern China.

Among the sacred mountains, Tai Shan is the most renowned and the most sacred. By the time Confucius reached its 5056-foot summit over 500 years B.C., the climb was already a venerable tradition. Confucius was much impressed by the view, and wrote of it in glowing terms. Since the Chinese have been quoting him on the subject ever since, it is likely that the name of Tai Shan has been known to more people down through the ages than that of any other mountain on earth. The town of Taian lies just at the foot of Tai Shan, and is on the main Peking-Shanghai rail line. A broad stone path with 6700 stone steps leads from the edge of town to the temple at the summit. In the old days, one could hire a sedan chair for the journey, but this form of exploitation of man by man has now been repudiated.

The famous mountain Omei Shan, south of Chengtu in

Szechuan Province, is at the eastern edge of the western Chinese highlands. However, rising as it does directly above the low, densely populated Szechuan basin, it is readily accessible to the lowland Chinese, who have traditionally considered it to be one of the sights of China Proper. In fact, among the mountains of eastern China, its fame is second only to that of Tai Shan. A stone path leads to Omei Shan's 9957-foot summit, where there is a temple. To most Chinese the only view from Omei Shan that deserves mention is to the east, out over the misty rice fields of Szechuan. But for mountain lovers another sight awaits them to the west: 100 miles away is the sharp white pyramid of 24,900-foot Minya Konka, rising above a land that is, or at least was, Tibetan in every respect but politically.

The highest peak in China Proper that is geomorphologically independent of the western Chinese ranges (that is to say excluding the Tsinling extension of the Kun Lun) is Wu Tai Shan (9971 feet) in Shansi Province, 180 miles west-southwest of Peking. The highest peak in the Tsinling is 13,474-foot Tai Pai Shan, 65 miles west-southwest of Hsian, in Shensi Province; the peak is situated at 108° longitude, and is the highest in China east of 105°.

▲ KOREA ▲

The mountains of Korea are usually thought of as a rough place to fight a war, and few indeed are the foreign visitors who have roamed the country's hills for pleasure. But there are fine mountains here and anyone with a climbing instinct who is stationed in Korea should consider himself lucky.

The highest mountain in Korea, 9003-foot Paektu-san, is on the border with China. It is a shield ("Hawaiian-type") volcano whose huge bulk covers a big slice of the border region. On the top of the mountain there is a caldera filled with a lake about six miles in circumference. The climb to the summit of Paektu-san is not technically difficult, but, at least before World War II, it took over a week. The government of North Korea has built new roads in the region, so the mountain is now without doubt more accessible (political considerations aside). In 1712, a Chinese and Korean expedition placed a boundary marker high on the mountain and may have reached the summit, but credit for the first verified ascent goes to Sir Francis Younghusband, whose climb in 1886 was in any case the first climb by a Westerner.

The most impressive mountains on the Korean peninsula are in the Taebaek Range, which parallels the east coast and straddles the Demilitarized Zone. To the north are the Diamond Mountains and to the south is Sorak-san. Both are areas of granite spires and cliffs right out of a Chinese painting. Sorak-san has recently been developed as a tourist center by the South Korean government, and offers fine opportunities for both hiking and rock climbing. The highest mountain in South Korea is Halla-san, the easily ascended 6398-foot volcano which crowns the island of Cheju-do.

The historic city of Seoul deserves mention as potentially one of the world's greatest urban rock-climbing centers. Right in the middle of town is Namsan, a 700-foot-high hill with cliffs made to order for practice rock climbs. From there, climbers can graduate to the rock peaks of Insupong, Dobong-san, Paegundae, and Obong-san, all within 10 miles of the city and easily accessible; none of these is over 2800 feet above sea level. Insupong is a steep rock dome with no easy way up, while Dobong-san has a sheer wall of firm granite nearly 1000 feet high.

▲ JAPAN ▲

Mt. Fuji

The most photographed, most painted, most climbed, and most looked at mountain on earth is Mt. Fuji (12,388 feet). Some people call it the most beautiful, but that of course depends on whether one's ideal of mountain beauty is ice-sheathed cragginess or symmetry and perfection of form.

MAP 42. MT. FUJI, JAPAN

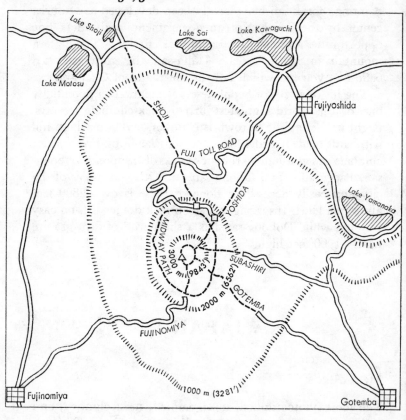

Scale 0 1 2 3 4 5 mi.

Fuji is one of the most perfect volcanic cones on earth, and by anyone's standards it is a very big mountain. Despite its relatively low elevation, as the world's mountains go, it rises 11,000 feet from its immediate base on the south, and 9000 feet above its base on the north. Mt. Fuji is now dormant, and the signs of vulcanism on the mountain itself are limited to a few small steam vents near the summit. However, there have been 18 eruptions in recorded history. The last, and one of the most destructive, occurred in 1707, at which time Tokyo, 50 miles away, was covered with six inches of ash. Each year during the official climbing season, July 1 through August 31, as many as 200,000 people climb Mt. Fuji. On a weekend there may be 20,000 climbers on the mountain, in an almost unbroken column from the bottom of the trail to the summit.

By the time Jacques Balmat and Dr. Paccard reached the summit of Mont Blanc in 1786—the first ascent of a major mountain in the Alps—the history of climbing on Mt. Fuji was about 1000 years old, and hundreds of thousands had already made the pilgrimage up its sacred slopes. The first ascent is not recorded, but probably occurred in the 8th or 9th century; a book that appeared in A.D. 850 contained a first-hand account of the crater. Some time before A.D. 1150 a Buddhist temple was constructed on the summit by a monk who had already climbed the mountain 100 times. After about 1550 there are reports of climbs by literary men, soldiers, and just plain tourists, in addition to the monks who for 700 years had been climbing the mountain to worship.

In 1558 the government issued an order stating that henceforth no more women would be allowed to climb Mt. Fuji, which indicates that they had up until then. Not until Lady

Parkes, the wife of the British Minister, made the climb in 1867 did any woman have the temerity to ignore the prohibition. The following year the ban was lifted, perhaps partly because the intrepid British lady had broken the spell. The first acent of Mt. Fuji by a foreigner was that of Sir Rutherford Alcock, the first British Minister to Japan, in 1860.

Three trails reach the summit of Mt. Fuji: Fujinomiya, from the south; Gotemba, from the east; and Yoshida, from the north. The Yoshida trail is joined by two other trails en route: Shoji and Subashiri. Each trail is divided into 10 sections marked by "stations," which have (or at least at one time had) huts. All the trails are in frequent use, but the great majority of hikers climb the Yoshida trail, because with the completion of the Fuji Toll Road on the north side of the mountain in 1963, it is now possible to drive or take a bus to the Yoshida 5th Station, at 7111 feet. From the end of the toll road the climb can easily be made in one day, but many hikers start late in the afternoon, spend the night at one of the upper stations, and complete the ascent early the next morning in time to see the sunrise from the summit. The Yoshida trail reaches the crater on the opposite side from the highest point, which is reached either by going clockwise around the rim, or by crossing the inside of the crater. On the highest point there is a weather observation station which is manned throughout the year. Elsewhere on the rim are several shrines, snack bars, huts, and even a post office.

From the summit a vast portion of Japan spreads out below. The ocean lies but 20 miles to the south, over an almost faultlessly even slope. To the north, one can see all the way to the Northern Alps, 100 miles away. Tokyo, to the east, is difficult to see during the day, but on a clear night the city's lights are easily visible. To enjoy the whole view, take the one-and-a-half mile trail around the rim of the crater.

Some people climb Mt. Fuji just for the fun of coming down. A broad cinder path for "screeing" (sliding on one's feet down a slope of small, loose pebbles) extends from the Yoshida 8th Station almost down to the road. There are also similar scree slides on the other routes, the best known being that of the Gotemba trail, where the slide runs from 10,000 feet all the way down to 4300 feet.

Although few hikers will require them, porters and guides are available; information about this can be obtained from tourist hotels at the base of the mountain. Also, horses are available for riding up to the 7th Station. Japanese tourists generally climb Mt. Fuji during the July 1–August 31 climbing season, because only then are the huts and other facilities in operation; however, there are no restrictions against climbing out-of-season. One advantage of climbing before or just after the official season is that the crowds are avoided, but climbers in June can expect to meet sizable patches of snow en route, while September climbers may encounter typhoons or early snowfall. The first winter climb of Mt. Fuji came in 1895, and now hundreds of climbers reach the top each winter; but Fuji in winter is no picnic, and climbers must be prepared for heavy snow and severe cold and wind.

Japan Alps

Mountaineering as a form of modern recreation did not begin in Japan until the 1890's, but in the short time since then, the Japanese have become the world's most enthusiastic mountain climbers. The figure 5,000,000 is sometimes given as a rough estimate of the country's climbing and mountain-hiking population, and a 1966 list of Japanese mountaineering clubs shows 317 in Tokyo alone. The most prestigious of these is the Japanese Alpine Club, No. 23, Nishiki-cho 3-chome, Kanda, Chiyoda-ku, Tokyo, which is also the club best qualified to assist foreign climbers.

Each year about 1,000,000 climbers visit the Northern Alps, which are Japan's most impressive nonvolcanic mountains. With this veritable flood of alpinists, it goes without saying that the range is not exactly a pristine wilderness. There are trails up all the peaks, and dozens of huts, with capacities ranging up to 600 people, are scattered all over the area. The climbing center for the Northern Alps is the resort of Kamikochi (5000 feet), which is three miles south of Oku-hotaka (10,466 feet), the highest peak in the range. Kamikochi is three hours by bus from Matsumoto, which is reached by train from Tokyo.

There are three trails to the summit of Oku-hotaka, the most popular of which is by way of the cirque of Karasawa on the mountain's northeast side. From Kamikochi the the climb is usually made in two days, spending the night at a hut en route. This route has no technical difficulties, but near the summit there is some steep scrambling with fixed cables at the tougher spots. For technical climbers, the rock walls of Oku-hotaka and its slightly lower satellite peaks provide some of the stiffest rock climbs in Japan. The view from Oku-hotaka is considered one of the finest in Japan. Far to the south on a clear day is Mt. Fuji, which looks sur-

MAP 43. MT. OKU-HOTAKA, JAPAN

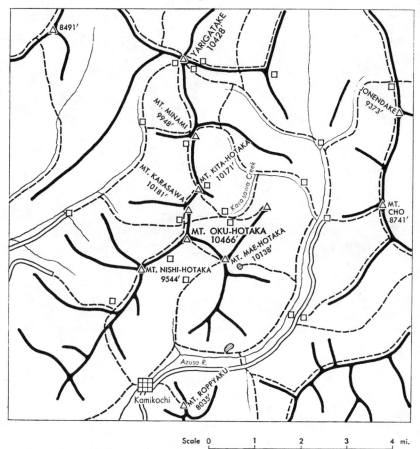

Scale 0   1   2   3   4 mi.

prisingly imposing from this distance. To the north, a three-mile-long ridge extends to the pointed peak of Yarigatake (10,428 feet), the second highest in the Northern Alps. The traverse of this ridge is perhaps the most popular route in the Alps. Yari also can be climbed in two days from Kamikochi; like Oku-hotaka, it is a steep scramble made easier by fixed cables.

Outside of the Kamikochi region, the favorite mountain of Japanese rock climbers in the Northern Alps is 9851-foot Tsurugi, near the northern end of the range. This is a very steep rock peak with both ridge and face climbs. Just the opposite sort of mountain awaits the hiker at the southern extremity of the range, where the isolated volcano Ontake, the second most sacred mountain in Japan, reaches 10,049 feet. Like Mt. Fuji, Ontake has been the goal of religious pilgrimages for many centuries, and it continues to be climbed by thousands of hikers each year; it is an easy one-day hike from Tanohara, which is two hours by bus from Fukushima.

The Northern Alps are situated between 36° and 37° north latitude, but they are more alpine than one would expect for mountains of their height at this latitude. Although there are no true glaciers, some of the heavy winter snowfall lasts through the summer; the highest peaks rise nearly 3000 feet above timberline. As on Mt. Fuji, the climbing season is essentially July and August, though some huts and hotels are open before and after the season. Climbing guides are available at Kamikochi.

The Northern Alps are just one of three ranges that make up the Japanese Alps. The other two are the Central Alps, just south of the Northern Alps; and the Southern Alps, which are southeast of the Central Alps. The highest peak in the Central Alps, 9697-foot Kiso-komagatake, is an easy one-day climb from Agematsu. The Southern Alps, though less majestic than the Northern, are an impressive range of mountains with something to offer both hikers and rock climbers. The highest peak in the Southern Alps, 10,472-foot Kitadake, and the second highest in all Japan, can be climbed in two days from Hirokawahara, which is reached by bus from Kofu.

Mt. Fuji and the Japanese Alps are both on Japan's main island, Honshu, which is mountainous from end to end. Another well-known mountain on Honshu is 6440-foot Tanigawa, which is noted for two things: first, it is a favorite weekend hiking and rock-climbing goal for residents of Tokyo (about four hours away by train); and second, it is the world's most murderous mountain, having claimed about 500 victims, mostly young, insufficiently experienced rock climbers. The highest peaks on the other important islands of Japan are 7513-foot Asahidake, on Hokkaido; 6499-foot Ishizuchizan, on Shikoku; and 5725-foot Kujusan, on Kyushu. All are popular hikes.

INDEX

BOOKS

from

THE MOUNTAINEERS

Climbers Guide to the Olympic Mountains
Cascade Alpine Guide: Climbing and High Routes, Columbia
      River to Stevens Pass
Cascade Alpine Guide: Climbing and High Routes, Stevens
      Pass to Rainy Pass
Snow Trails: Ski and Snowshoe Routes in the Cascades
Mountaineering: The Freedom of the Hills
Medicine for Mountaineering
Mountaineering First Aid
Snowshoeing
The South Cascades: The Gifford Pinchot National Forest
Challenge of Mount Rainier
The Unknown Mountain
Fire and Ice: The Cascade Volcanoes
Across the Olympic Mountains: The Press Expedition
Men, Mules and Mountains: Lieutenant O'Neil's Olympic
      Expeditions
The Coffee Chased Us Up: Monte Cristo Memories
Challenge of the North Cascades
Bicycling Notes
Hiking Notes
Climbing Notes
Northwest Trees
The Ascent of Denali
Canoe Routes: Yukon Territory
Canoe Routes: British Columbia